Touching *the* Wild U.P.

Outdoors Adventures in

Michigan's Upper Peninsula

Dad,
Thank you for always
encouraging us to explore and roamin
the wilderness!
Love, Wendi and Sara

John Highlen And
Dale, Kole, Andrew,
Allagash, and Milada ☺

NATURAL CONNECTIONS
Deerton, Michigan

Fulton Books, Inc.
Meadville, PA

Published by Fulton Books 2021

ISBN 978-1-63710-543-6 (paperback)
ISBN 978-1-63710-544-3 (digital)

Printed in the United States of America

This book is dedicated to my parents, for supporting my adventurous spirit and giving me room to roam.

We cannot all live in the wilderness, or even close to it, but we can, no matter where we spend our lives, remember the background which shaped this sense of the eternal rhythm, remember that days, no matter how frenzied their pace, can be calm and unhurried.
—Sigurd F. Olson

Contents

Acknowledgements

A special thank-you to Ashley Tyler and the staff at Fulton Books for all of their help and guidance. Also, thank-you to Stu Osthoff, at The Boundary Waters Journal, for giving me honest feedback on some of my early writing—Sometimes, hard knocks provide the best education.

I very much appreciate my family and friends for sharing in many of the adventures that led to this book. And, a special thank-you to my wife, Julie, for lending her artistic talents to this project with the watercolor painting that adorns the cover and the pen & ink drawings introducing each chapter.

I'm indebted to my dad for igniting the flame of my outdoors passion. Though he's been gone for many years and no longer shares in my adventures, I take him with me still.

Most importantly, I thank God for the natural wonders of creation that are ours to explore, enjoy and care for.

INTRODUCTION

One of the great things about the Upper Peninsula is that, no matter where you are, you're usually not more than a few minutes away from experiencing nature's wildness—maybe not pure wilderness, but wildness. This is true even in towns and "cities." Whether it's a shoreline stretch of one of our surrounding Great Lakes, a scenic trail, a quiet inland lake, a mesmerizing river, or an inviting forest, they're all readily within reach and waiting to stimulate our senses.

With its vast forests and untamed waters, in some ways, the Upper Peninsula has a certain restlessness about it, making you feel like you need to stay on the move so as not to miss anything. Then again, those same characteristics sometimes envelop your senses and emotions to the point where you don't want to move or even blink so as not to lose that moment. My transition to being a full-time Yooper and becoming part of the landscape has spanned some fifty years. Mentally, I think I moved here years ago. It just took the rest of me a while to catch up.

My interactions with the UP's wild spirit started during family vacations in my childhood. I remember wandering bare dirt trails at Tahquamenon Falls State Park and venturing out onto rock formations right next to the falls in the days before there were boardwalks and viewing platforms. At Fort Wilkins State Park, we woke up to our pop-up camper moving around as a large black bear tried to dig our cooler out from underneath it. I recall looking down from the escarpment at Lake of the Clouds in the Porcupine Mountains and wondering what adventures lay hidden in the vast forest stretching out in front of me. I yearned to explore that winding ribbon of water flowing from the lake. In those days, the UP was a far-off world of dreams, visited only occasionally on those summer vacations.

College years were spent engrossed in the Keweenaw while attending Michigan Technological University. That was when the snowshoes my parents had given me for Christmas when I was twelve years old were finally put to use in snow depths worthy of them. I caught Superior salmon off the breakers at the west end of Portage Canal and hunted snowshoe hares for the first time in my life. Though my primary focus was the close-at-hand Keweenaw, through hunting, fishing, ice climbing, rock climbing, and cross-country skiing, a friend and I managed to explore those vast forests of the Porkies, and I got an up-close look at that ribbon of water flowing from Lake of the Clouds.

Building a rustic log cabin in the Tahquamenon area early in my married life provided a whole new base for my UP explorations that continue even today.

Now, in my later years, I'm blessed to be living here year-round and experiencing most of everything the UP wilds have to offer. Even though I get outside and play in the wilds often, my outdoor adventure to-do list is still growing instead of shrinking. The more I learn and experience, the more I want to experience.

This book is a collection of those experiences, touching on everything from wild patches along beaten paths to true wilderness adventures. My hope is that these tales will not only help you appreciate the wild UP but also encourage you to venture out and mingle with it yourself.

John Muir said, "Everybody needs beauty as well as bread, places to play in and pray in, where nature may heal and cheer and give strength…"

Well, between wilderness areas, national forests, state land, and timber company land, the Upper Peninsula boasts of millions of acres of publicly available land. There are roughly 1,700 miles of Great Lakes shoreline, 4,300 inland lakes, and 12,000 miles of streams. The UP includes 29 percent of Michigan's land mass and only about 3 percent of Michigan's population. So there's plenty of room to play, whether that means hunting, fishing, hiking, camping, skiing, snowshoeing, paddling, climbing, bird watching, or just breathing some fresh north woods air. If you're looking for a natural prayer chapel, there are awesome hemlock cathedrals, soul-stirring waterfalls, and Great Lakes vistas that will leave you at a loss for words.

Aristotle noted, "In anything of nature there is something of the marvelous." Here in the wild Upper Peninsula, you're likely to find yourself wondering how the marvelous can be so common.

John Highlen
October 2020
Deerton, Michigan

DOUBLE-DIGIT DREAMS

Trout are miracles. Each one individually painted by God and given a character all their own. In some ways, trout are trout, but then again, each one is a unique creature here for a brief time to enrich this grand drama of life. They are the essence of wild. To be connected to one by a delicate strand is to feel the pulse of wilderness.

Overcast skies and a cool, stiff breeze didn't make the day feel much like late August, but being in the Upper Peninsula of Michigan, not far from the Lake Superior shoreline, it wasn't exactly abnormal either. My wife, Julie, and I were debating whether or not it would be worth setting up her booth at the Munising Farmer's and Artisan's Market to sell her paintings. A quick phone call confirmed

JOHN HIGHLEN

our suspicions that the Pictured Rocks boat tours were cancelled due to the waves, so we decided to skip the market and get other things done. For Julie, that meant painting. For me, it meant playing in the water—playing as in chasing after wild trout with a fly rod as opposed to simply frolicking and splashing about. The trout often do some splashing, but if I'm splashing about, it usually means there's been an incident, which I'd rather not write about.

Like a grade-schooler sprung free by the recess bell, I was out the door and headed for one of my favorite local brook trout haunts, a place where I knew I could quickly get to some decently fishable water without a lot of fanfare or bushwhacking. For various reasons (none of them good, I might add), I hadn't been there in a few weeks, so I was surprised at how shallow the water was. Beneath the bridge that I usually waded under was a three-foot-wide exposed sand bank to walk on, and just upstream, the normally shin-deep water rolling over a rippled sandstone slab barely wet my ankles. The first bend hole, where I usually started fishing, resembled more of a minor pocket than a true hole, and the couple of small fish it held were as spooky as a caffeinated red squirrel.

I began to get concerned, hoping the local trout population was doing well despite the shortage of water. I was also a bit concerned about how good the fishing might not be. The thought of turning back in order to spare myself from the likelihood of an unsuccessful outing briefly entered my mind, but I dismissed it before it had a chance to sabotage my afternoon. The fact that I was chasing wild trout in a cold, clean north woods stream already made for a successful adventure and a well-spent afternoon, so I had nothing to lose.

Stalking farther upstream, I spotted two fish under some low overhanging tag alder branches, so I stopped and watched, trying to evaluate the possibilities of me getting a fly in to them. A few minutes of observation revealed a couple more larger fish, including what was clearly a nice rainbow about twelve inches long. Before launching my first cast, I had spotted eight or nine fish under those branches. Two were no doubt rainbows. The others looked and acted trouty, but I wasn't quite sure. Something was slightly different. Still, I figured I would catch first and answer questions later.

I had already tied on a Parachute Adams because that was what caught my eye when I opened my fly box. The first few casts fell short due to my subconscious aversion to decorating the overhanging branches guarding the fish. A couple of casts did hit leaves, but I was able to free them without scattering fish or losing my fly. Any time my fly landed even close to the spot I had mentally dubbed ideal, several extra-small fish would immediately go on the attack like small bluegills nibbling on a worm before anything of any size had a chance to even give it a look. After fifteen or twenty minutes of casting practice and teasing the fry, I finally managed to hook a seven-incher. The excitement was short-lived, as I soon realized it was a rainbow chub, not a rainbow trout. Assuming the rest of the slightly peculiar trout were also chubs, I decided to move on because I had told my wife I'd only be a few hours and my watch seemed to be spinning in high gear, a phenomenon I experience quite often in my fishing pursuits.

Just up around the next bend was a long, normally dark hole that was my ultimate destination for the evening. It had a vertical sandstone ledge guarding one side only a few feet from the opposite bank. A few strategically placed branches made it maddeningly difficult to drop a fly where it needed to be. Somehow, the fish seemed to know that. I had fished this hole with a bead-head nymph a few times the previous year, unsuccessfully, but I couldn't figure out exactly what was going on due to my inability to actually see what was down in the hole in the way of either fish or structure. Now the water was much shallower, making visibility in the hole like looking into a relatively small aquarium. I cautiously approached the tail of the hole to a point where I was looking at the end of the submerged ledge. Several smaller trout were clearly visible, lined up along the base of the ledge. Near the head of the hole was a stark cream-colored patch of sand where the river entered the hole from a sharp bend to the left. Just beyond the bright sand patch was a collection of logs of various sizes and orientations. As I watched, a few trout in the eight-inch range cruised across the sandy patch, looking almost black against the bleached sand. Brookies, no doubt. *Salvelinus fontinalis*. The main reason for my visit.

I switched to a red Copper John because nothing was rising and brookies are rumored to like red. I've never actually substantiated that rumor, but I've never heard it ridiculed either, so I take it as somewhat of a truth. Several casts resulted in the number 14 nymph swirling harmlessly through the hole about halfway up in the water column. Obviously, even with much shallower water than normal, there were some squirrely currents in there messing with my fly. I began to understand my previous lack of success in such a promising-looking hole. I added another small split shot a foot above the fly. In the next cast, the split shot slid down the line before the nymph even hit the water. Three small fish picked at the sinker just to insult me. I slid it back in place and snugged it down with a firmer bite from my front teeth.

It's probably not the best technique, but that's how I've always done it, and it works well. I've yet to experience any ill effects from biting sinkers, so I'm not too inclined to change. I just assume my immune system is up to the challenge.

The follow-up cast landed on a branch and wrapped itself around a few times just to ensure there would be no way to unsnag it. After muttering a remark I'll claim I don't remember, I broke off the Copper John and tied on a different nymph. It was something tannish, as I recall. Probably a Hare's Ear or maybe an orange Hot Belly.

A touch more line sent the next cast a little farther up toward the head of the hole. Apparently, the slight plop of the sinker entering the water drew attention because an eighteen-inch rainbow torpedoed from the scattering of logs straight at my fly. In the glass-clear water, it was like watching the action on television. Smaller fish scattered as the rainbow slashed twice at the little nymph and missed. Then I watched the white mouth open wide and clamp down on my fly very matter-of-factly. The fish turned abruptly and cruised toward the sandstone ledge, my line trailing from the corner of its mouth.

After snapping out of my momentary stun, I lifted the rod tip and saw the rainbow flinch slightly as I set the small hook, then watched as it began circling the hole like it was trying to figure out a plan. As my mind began to slow down a bit from the initial flurry of action, the realization that I actually had an eighteen-inch trout on my line finally set in. I had read about this sort of thing before but never actually experienced it myself. Of course, it finally happened when there were no witnesses around. That seems to be when a lot of the bigger fish are caught.

My first real fly-fishing encounter with big fish had taken place the previous season on the Carp River. I had just caught a couple of small rainbows, so I was beginning to relax and get into a fly-fishing mindset, looking at the world through fishy eyes. Just above a pretty little inlet creek, I found a moderately deep hole, lined on the near-side with large rocks. The head of the hole was a fast white chute between boulders, funneling in a steady supply of oxygen and food. My Pheasant Tail nymph made the journey through the shadowed hole several times unmolested. As I was preparing to roll-cast to the white chute, I saw him. Well, whether him or her, I didn't know, and it really didn't matter. It was a fish. A nice fish. A real nice fish by my standards. I'd estimate it at around twenty inches. It was a trout fisherman's trout. The number 14 nymph wasn't going to get it anymore. This called for something meaty, like a streamer. I stepped back away from the hole and pulled out my box of streamers. My first choice was a Mickey Finn, but when I tried to thread the tippet, I found the eye was plugged with excess glue from a sloppy tying job. For some reason, instead of just quickly using the point of another hook to clean out the eye, I pulled out a Muddler Minnow instead. My brain was apparently a little too rattled for complex thinking.

Excited fingers don't tie on new flies very well, especially when the eyes they're partnered with keep glancing back at the river through the blur of a flip-down magnifier. The second try was the charm. Easing back out toward the hole, I saw it again—this time, more clearly—as it swirled and cruised the far edge of the hole in shallower water. And it wasn't alone. There were two. The second one was a bit bigger and darker. I sent in the Muddler. Again and again, I sent in the Muddler. Nothing. I stood motionless for a few minutes, just studying the dark water. That was when I caught another glimpse. They were still there despite my repeated trolling.

Henry David Thoreau is credited with saying that many men go fishing their entire lives without knowing it is not fish they are after. Well, maybe so. At times. I mean, most times, I do enjoy just being on the water, exploring the stream, pondering its mysteries, listening to the wild. Actually catching fish is an unnecessary bonus. Other times, not. There are days when I want to catch a fish so bad that I'd consider shaving the fur and feathers off a fly and using the hook to impale a worm found under a streamside log. I've never actually done it, mind you. It's just a thought, but on those days, I'm after fish. This was becoming one of those days.

Two roll casts later, I felt a slight tug on the line, followed by the pulsing of a six-inch rainbow trout, which I quickly landed and released. Repeatedly, I swung the Muddler through the hole, but another six-inch rainbow was all I connected with. The two big fish of my dreams never showed up again. I suspected they were probably sulking somewhere in the bottom of the hole, waiting for the muddling to stop.

Eventually, I had to pack up and move on, but I was a changed man. I still enjoyed the pleasure of willing eight-inch brookies, but now double-digit-sized fish would forever swirl in the back of my mind.

Coming back to my present fish, as I watched the rainbow circling the hole, trailing my line, I wished I had been using a bigger fly with a bigger hook, but I thought I was fishing for eight-inch brook trout, not an eighteen-inch energized torpedo. The four-weight rod was bent nicely. To my surprise, the 7x tippet was doing fine. Not being experienced at events like this, I got antsy to bring the fish to the net. It seemed willing to succumb until I tried to move the net into position. The spotted steely head shook violently as the fish spun and made a dash toward the scattered logs. I saw my fly shooting through the water toward me after popping loose from the bony jaw. With a flash of its tail, the fish was gone. I suspected it buried itself back into the pile of logs, but I didn't actually see it because I was too busy still looking at the place where it used to be.

I suppose a deflating disappointment should have set in, but strangely, it didn't. I read somewhere that the most vivid memories are of the ones that got away. All I can say to that observation is "Amen!" Later that night, as I lay in bed, I could still see every slow-motion detail of that encounter, especially that big white mouth gaping open just before it clamped down on my fly.

After a few minutes of staring at the logs, I cast again with the same fly. Some little ones poked at it, like little ones do. A few casts later, an eight-inch brook trout pulsed at the end of the line. This one came to my net with sunset belly and haloed spots. I held it in the water and admired its wildness for a few seconds. Then I opened my hand. The brookie eased forward a foot or so, then sat there for a moment, finning, looking like a magazine photo. I watched its greenish worm-tracked back cruise over to the sandstone ledge and tuck itself into an undercut.

I knew it was time to be getting home for dinner, but I excitedly sent another cast toward the middle of the hole. It was intercepted by one of those strategically placed branches. In my hurried attempt to free it, the 7x tippet popped, as I should've expected. As I pondered the limp end of my remaining tippet, I decided that was my queue to head for home. The eight-inch brookie was still visible under the ledge as I reeled in and slowly headed downstream. I paused on the way to watch the group of chubs and the twelve-inch rainbow still tucked under their protective tag alder canopy. After briefly entertaining the idea of a cast, I decided I'd had enough piscatorial taunting for one day.

There wasn't much I could add to the day anyway. Clear shallow water, an overcast sky, and several fish had all played their part in moving me up a rung or two on the fly-fishing ladder of experience. Considering the fact that my first trout on a fly could have swam laps in a standard drinking glass, I had made considerable progress. I didn't have any big-fish pictures from my latest adventure, but I did have some vivid footage swirling around between my ears.

Dinner was waiting at home, and I had stories to share at the table.

THE FALLS

*Moving water beckons. The music is irresistible. We need to see
it, eagerly navigating woods and fields, trailing the sound to its
source. The flow is tranquil, powerful, mesmerizing, as it erodes
earth and polishes rock. Peacefully relentless, doing what it does;
harboring wild fish and wild dreams, carrying away today's concerns
and dissolving tomorrow's. To ride its current is to flow with life.
Attach your mind to one of its flowing molecules and you can tour
the world, for each molecule of water, in its varying phases, may
travel to the far reaches of the earth or the limits of the atmosphere
and back, to once again sing its chorus in a north woods stream.*

In the eastern Upper Peninsula, "the falls" typically refers to
Tahquamenon. I remember visiting there as a kid in the 1970s
when the trails were paved in dirt and there were no viewing decks

or barriers. I have a picture from the 1960s of my dad sitting on a log sticking out over the upper falls—not a good idea and probably one of the reasons there are now railings and fences in most areas. Even though there are now paved walkways, boardwalks, viewing platforms, railings, and fences to reduce erosion and environmental damage (as well as make things safer and improve accessibility), some things haven't changed. The roughly five-mile trail between the upper and lower falls is still an unsmoothed earth trail with rocks and roots and even some good old mudholes. Autumn colors are vibrant as ever, and spring flowers still carpet the forest floor. The raw, roaring power of Tahquamenon is still there too. As I stand on a viewing platform, staring into the rushing amber current, I feel its wild and untamed spirit as much as when I was a kid. Maybe even more so. Conservationist and outdoors adventure author Sigurd Olson referred to this child-like sense of wonder as hearing the pipes of Pan, referring to those elfin notes of Peter Pan. To me, those notes are ever present in every waterfall I see.

Central and western UP waterfalls are nearly countless when you consider all the small creeks that thread their way across the landscape. In fact, we have several small falls of around twelve inches right on our own property. These miniature drops may not exude roaring power, but they stir something in me just the same. Laughing Whitefish, Rock River, Chapel, Mosquito, Miner's, Munising, Hungarian, Manganese, Jacob's, Silver, Montreal, Wagner, Carp River, Yellow Dog, Eagle River, Scott—whether a step-out-of-the-car roadside novelty or a true backcountry experience, they hold the same wild allure falling water always does. There are entire guide books written about UP waterfalls, which is why many of the falls now have well-trampled trails leading to them. Regardless, many of the falls still have no paved paths, railings, or fences, and viewing platforms are typically whichever rock you choose to stand on. Those unhindered ones that allow an intimate connection are some of my personal favorites.

I love to fish near waterfalls. There is something about fishing below falls that makes the fishing seem wilder and more adventurous, maybe even a little exotic. Sometimes the fishing is good. Other times, it's just the scenery and atmosphere that are good. Either way, there's something to be said about fishing near waterfalls. In the UP, below major plunges, you typically find rainbows or a mix of trout. Above is normally brook trout territory. I'm sure there are exceptions, but that's the general rule. I've found it to be the case with several waterfalls that I have fished near.

I spent some time fishing the pool below Yellow Dog Falls one time, while my wife, Julie, worked on some plein air painting nearby. After several fruitless fly changes, I decided it was one of those days— you know, the type of day that's probably better spent taking pictures or daydreaming than fishing. Regardless, it was a fitting place for any of those activities.

I've heard it said that, in Maine, if you dump a five-gallon bucket of water in the woods, you will soon have brook trout in the puddle. I don't know that brookies are quite that abundant here in the UP, above or below waterfalls, but a couple of years ago, after a few fishless hours of exploring Silver Creek on opening day, as I was heading back to my truck, I ran across a six-inch brookie in an eight-inch-wide run-off that was flowing down the middle of the trail. After entertaining the idea of letting it calm down for a few minutes then trying to get it to take a fly, I decided that probably wasn't a very sporting thing to do.

One of my favorite parts of exploring UP backcountry is finding unnamed waterfalls. Many are in the one-foot to four-foot range, but I have found them ten feet high or more as well. Whether in the middle of a designated wilderness area, out in a national forest, or on timber company forest reserve land (CFR), most of these surprises are seldom visited, at least not by people. In fact, many are unknown or at least forgotten by a vast majority of the population. That brings to mind that old philosophical question about if a tree falls in the forest and nobody is there, does it make a sound? The underlying question, of course, is that if it's not in the presence of people or if it doesn't really affect people, does it really matter? The short answer or at least my short answer is "Absolutely!" If you consider every little detail of everything that happens in this world, then most events are outside of the witness or recognition of people. Expand that thought to the entire universe, and things that people actually witness or are mindful of constitute a minute percentage of the grand sum of events or objects or beings. Many of those things that most people are not even aware of are the very things that allow the universe, including our world, to function. Those are the things that make exploring fun and rewarding.

Getting back to the discussion at hand, little-known or unknown waterfalls certainly fall into that category. I have had the pleasure of visiting roughly a hundred waterfalls of various sizes across the Upper Peninsula. Nobody but God knows how many there actually are, so I will always have the possibility of discovering another one on any given adventure, which, again, is part of what makes exploring so much fun.

Moving water attracts people. It plays with their imagination and sparks their curiosity. Falling water even more so. Moving water is part of us. It runs through us. It literally feeds the source of our thoughts—that mass that rattles around in our cranium. Like a beaver attracted to the sound of water rushing through a breach in their dam, I am pulled in by the sound of rushing water. Once I hear it, I just have to check it out. More often than not, the sound of rushing water leads to a small cascade or just some fast water in a small creek, but sometimes it leads me to a plunge.

When we first moved to the UP a few years ago, I set out to explore a small creek that runs through a nearby parcel of CFR land. Shortly after leaving the road, I could hear it. The audible intensity spoke of more than mere running water. I could hear the churning of a plunge pool in the spring-melt flow. Homing in on the call, I splashed my way through the soggy late-March woods. The swollen creek poured over a large boulder and landed on another, probably three feet below. The tannin-laden water roiled and foamed like Tahquamenon. I'm sure others know about this neighborhood spectacle, but I have visited numerous times and have never even seen footprints, let alone actually bumping into someone else during my stay. That's the beauty of little special places like that. You can feel like they are your personal place, your secret hangout. So can numerous other people.

I know of a couple of wilderness area waterfalls in the ten-foot category that are like that. I stumbled onto them while hunting a couple of Novembers ago. I'm sure other people know about them, but you can't tell by the surrounding woods or lack of any access trail. In my mind, those falls are my secret. They're my personal wilderness retreat for exotic fishing and untethered dreaming. I rarely go there, but then again, part of the fun is that I know that I can.

One of the other engaging things about waterfalls is that they are always in flux, always changing. Depending on season and weather conditions, they can be a raging torrent capable of claiming lives or a delicate trickle singing their melody as a hesitant whisper. Laughing Whitefish Falls, which is not far from my house based on river miles, roars as it drops snowmelt and spring showers for some eighty feet. Late summer or early autumn, when clouds have been frugal with their showers, it's a thin veil sliding down layered, moss-covered bedrock, calling like a breeze through the forest.

A couple of years ago, Julie and I were on the Pictured Rocks lakeshore section of the North Country Trail, hiking in from the west to see Bridalveil Falls, and found that there was a new waterfall a little before we reached Bridalveil. The creek feeding the new falls was running right down the North Country Trail before dropping over the cliff into Superior. As I neared the new falls, I walked into a steady rain shower, which caught me by surprise. The rain was isolated to a small area right near the top of the falls. Another strange thing about the rain was that the air didn't smell like rain. As soon as it starts raining, the air takes on a somewhat pungent, earthy kind of smell. I used to think it was just the smell of wet soil, but then I noticed that the smell was the same no matter what type of soil was around. It also smells the same when it rains early in the spring, when snow still covers the ground, so it's not likely just the smell of wet soil. I speculate that maybe it's what clouds smell like and the raindrops carry the scent of the clouds. Regardless of what causes that typical rain smell, it wasn't there. After seriously looking things over (and getting wet), I realized that the wind was picking up spray from the falls, lifting it well overhead and dropping it back onto the top of the falls. The falls were basically raining on themselves. That phenomenon held my attention long enough that we ended up not having time to make it over to Bridalveil that evening.

A couple of weeks later, we approached Bridalveil from the east and found that a beaver (or beavers) had built a dam in the creek feeding Bridalveil. There was enough water flowing over and through the dam to continue feeding Bridalveil, and the pond the dam created was spilling out of the west end of its pocket and eventually running down the trail to create the new falls that had rained on me. I say it rained on *me* because Julie was smart enough to stay out of the rain.

A lot of the waterfalls around Munising are nice, and it's fun to take a look every now and then just because, but all the railings and viewing platforms make them somehow seem more tame. I fully understand and appreciate the reasons for such structures and associated rules, but it certainly takes away from the experience. It's like going to a zoo. You get to see the animals, but it's not complete reality. Seeing a bear or a moose in a zoo, for instance, doesn't even compare to seeing them in the uncaged wild. I have encountered both at pretty close range in the wild, and it's a whole different encounter than when you are on the other side of a fence. Waterfalls don't get caged in, but when I am on a viewing platform, behind a railing or fence, I feel a little like I'm caged in, or maybe it's more like I'm caged out. Regardless, I don't feel like I get as much from the experience.

That's probably why I like falls like Rock River Falls so much. They're not as tall as, say, Laughing Whitefish or Munising Falls, and they don't possess the raw, thunderous power of Tahquamenon, but being in a designated wilderness area, they too are wild. They're not behind railings or fences, and you are not limited to the view from a designated platform. You can get up close and personal from any view you choose. Every time we visit, I carefully walk around the plunge pool into the mist and stick my hand into the fringe of the falls just because I can, because I appreciate being able to do it. That, and the kid in me just can't resist it—the kid that has always loved to be able to reach out and touch the wild.

Montreal Falls, in the Keweenaw, is also in that wide-open, unfettered category. The lower falls tumble directly into Lake Superior to begin the 130-year journey to the St. Mary's River. Of course, that timing supposes that water actually stays in Superior for the entire time that it takes the lake to turn over. If it evaporates and reenters Superior as rain or snow, only to repeat the cycle, there's no telling how long the journey will take or ultimately where it goes.

Getting back to the falls, they are as wild, uncaged, and available for up-close, hands-on enjoyment as any I have seen. Being that they roil directly into Superior, they're intriguing to fish in because you never know exactly what you may catch. Depending on the time of year, lake trout, steelhead, coho, splake, and coaster brook trout are all real possibilities, along with a host of other potential surprises. And if you're looking for more adventure, go farther a few bends, and a fifteen-minute walk upstream brings you to the upper falls plunging through a rocky chute where, again, the only things limiting access are trees and rocks. Safety notwithstanding, the entire area is open to enjoy from pretty much any vantage point that strikes your fancy. Last time I fished the lower falls, Superior was too high for me to wade in to where I could reach some of the best spots, but I did manage to catch a sucker and locate a couple of leaks in my waders.

The first time I fished the bottom of the lower falls, when I reeled in and got out of the water to leave, a young guy stepped into my place and proceeded to run an imitation spawn through a churning chute right near shore. As I was packing up, he hooked a nice firm fish about twelve inches long. I couldn't resist going over to take a look. We were having a difficult time deciding whether it was an honest-to-goodness coaster brook trout or a splake. It was either a coaster with a slight fork in its tail or a splake with a little less fork than usual. We never reached a conclusion, but the foot of a cascading waterfall churning into Lake Superior in the middle of a wide-open stretch of wild shoreline is a great place to have a conversation like that—or any conversation, for that matter.

Canyon Falls on Baraga County's Sturgeon River is another wide-open falls adventure. The main falls are about twenty feet high, which in itself isn't necessarily spectacular, but they pour into the beginning of a canyon ranging from probably thirty to sixty feet deep. The combination of rapids, cascades, runs, and pools stretching through what seems like at least a quarter-mile of dark mossy canyon walls with feeder creeks and periodic chutes accessing the river provides a wild flair.

The first time my wife and I explored the area, I was surprised to find so much wild, churning water and untamed cliffs with virtually no railings or barriers other than one small particularly dangerous area. As we followed the canyon lip, poking our heads over now and then to witness the energy and look for photo opportunities, we came across a group of young people that looked like they were teenagers. That estimate may be in question, though, because I'm getting to the age where most people under the age of thirty look like a teenager. I've seen police officers that I doubted were out of high school, and every so often, when I see a sign at the grocery store stating the birth year for legal alcohol purchases, I find myself doing the math to convince myself that year was actually twenty-one years ago.

Anyway, it caught me by surprise when I noticed the kids were wet. We peeked over the probably thirty-foot cliff as one of them took the plunge into the pool below. About that time, another one popped up out of the canyon after having climbed back up the rock. While I was in the middle of thinking through all the reasons that jumping off of a thirty-foot cliff into a relatively small-looking river pool then scrambling back up the cliff with wet bare feet wasn't a very sane thing to be doing, the realization hit me that thirty-five or forty years ago, I would have probably been the next one in line. The more I thought about it as we watched and listened to the laughter and joking around, the more I admired their youthful and maybe even a bit naive sense of adventure. Deep down, part of me wanted to join in, but I wasn't dressed for it and didn't have a towel, which I then realized wouldn't have mattered forty years ago. I ultimately didn't take the plunge, but the opportunity is still open.

Thinking of all the rivers and little unnamed creeks with unnamed falls of various sizes across the Upper Peninsula, there is no telling how many are out there to be discovered (or maybe rediscovered), explored, and enjoyed. So there are plenty of opportunities still open. That's part of the wonder and beauty of this wild place we call the UP.

CAMP STATE OF MIND

*In the North Woods, Camp is as much a state of mind as
a physical place. Camp and a camp state of mind support
each other...or, maybe feed off of each other. Regardless,
the reality of Camp is what we imagine it to be.*

A common condition among many Yoopers is having a camp.
Regardless of what it means elsewhere, here in the UP, a camp
is pretty much anyplace other than your actual residence where you
go to enjoy the outdoors and get away from things. It's a place to
get away and relax in the woods or along the water. It's a place to
reconnect with reality, with life, and with the earth—a place where
we can take a deep breath and open our eyes and minds and hearts

to resync whatever's off-kilter and get back on track with things that really matter. Some camps are rustic hunting or fishing camps with not much in the way of amenities. Others are family retreats, often located on a body of water, that you might expect to see in the pages of some high-end, glossy magazine. Still others truly are camps, complete with an old camper trailer or even a tent.

We've owned our camp since 1993. The dream of having a getaway in the north woods started long before that, but I can't recall exactly when. That first year of owning the place, it was truly a camp in every sense of the word. We bought the property—eighty acres of mostly woods—during the summer and pitched our family tent there for a few days in late September. As I recall, on the second day, a light morning drizzle turned into wet snow by late afternoon. We have a picture of our youngest daughter, who was less than a year old, in her walker, bundled up in a snowsuit and boots. Our oldest daughter, who was three, didn't seem to care about the weather conditions as long as we still got to read stories in the tent before bedtime.

After that adventure, I decided a cabin needed to be a sooner-than-later addition, so we put a plan in action that winter. A cabin built of logs was the only option I ever considered. The beauty of a log cabin is that, even indoors, you're still surrounded by trees. Since its inception, our family has simply referred to it as "the cabin," whether we were talking about the actual building, the land it sits on, or both. Now the term is so engrained in us, we still just refer to it as *the cabin*, even though we now know better. The term *camp* just hasn't caught on with us yet.

We were living downstate at the time, a seven-hour drive from our UP property. A neighbor had a stand of mature red pines out back on their farm, and they wanted some fire trails cut through them. Another neighbor (neighbor by UP standards, meaning they lived within ten miles or so) had a portable sawmill and some time on his hands due to work issues. He lived in a small log home he had built himself, so he had a good idea of what I needed for the job. We made a deal—scribbled on a sheet of notebook paper and sealed with a handshake—that he would fell the trees, cut them into sixteen-foot sections, and saw a flat on two sides, making all the logs six inches thick (more or less). I would take it from there.

Once I had all the logs, which was about three hundred pieces, I acquired a couple of old drawknives from an antique shop and started skinning the bark off. I bought antique tools because, at that point, I didn't know new tools like that were even available. I have no idea if new tools would have been cheaper or not, but it turned out to be more of a novel adventure with antique tools anyway. It took me a good share of the winter to get all the logs skinned, working only nights and weekends, and I remember my Carhartt overalls being pretty sappy by the time I was done with all the bark removal. They acted as a giant pine-scented air freshener in our entryway, where I hung them, which was a nice fringe benefit. My typical night was to head out to our pole barn around 9:00 p.m. and work until 11:00 p.m. or midnight. Surprisingly, there weren't any major mishaps, but a few times during single-digit temperatures, I did chip the knife blades on frozen knots. They still work fine, though, and I've actually used them on a few other small projects over the years.

Once all the bark was off, I'd stack the logs in a pile to dry, with air gaps between each log and each layer. In May, I cut a tongue-and-groove template out of plywood and started building cabin walls in my pole barn, using a chainsaw to cut the joints. I ended up building the complete 20 × 24 cabin base—8.5 feet high walls—inside my barn, which invoked some interesting comments from friends when they stopped by to take a look. "What the…?" and "Holy crap!" were common statements. The whole thing seemed normal to me.

Why not build a log cabin from scratch in your barn, then dismantle it, haul it up north, hand-carry it to a building site, and reassemble it on a remote eighty-acre chunk of woods in the UP? Nothing out of the ordinary about that. Of course, when I was a kid, I'd sleep in my pup tent in the backyard during Christmas break, and in college, I would sleep in a cave in a Lake Superior cliff so I could ice-climb all weekend, so my view of normal might be a little skewed from everyone else's. Anyway, who's to say?

In July, I hand-drove a fifty-eight-foot deep well in order to have enough water to mix ready-mix cement for footings, which consisted of twenty individual pylons to support the cabin and porch. I hand-dug all the footings roughly six feet deep and hand-mixed the cement because that's the way I do things—difficult. Plus, I was trying to keep expenses down, and my labor was considerably cheaper than renting equipment.

By August, I was ready to begin final construction. I hadn't pre-planned a construction crew, so I was relieved when several people volunteered on their own. I wasn't sure if they really wanted to help or if they just wanted to see first-hand how this whole thing panned out. Then, of course, there was also the epic adventure aspect of the project. People tend to be drawn to epic adventures, if for no other reason than the novelty of it. I'm guessing that came into play at least a little. Besides, it would make for a great story to tell their friends.

The crew consisted of two of my uncles, Frank and Art, my brother-in-law Doug, and family friends Ken and Marg. My friend Rod hauled the cabin logs and other building supplies with his semi and flatbed trailer. A mutual friend, Dan, went along for the ride with Rod. Based on Dan's comments when they arrived at our property ten miles down a seasonal sand "road," I don't think he knew what he was getting into. Actually, I'm not sure any of us did. Even years later, the mere mention of our cabin would send Dan into a well-animated storytelling frenzy.

The entire construction plan was in my head. Being that I was a lot younger then, relying on my memory for cabin details wasn't as iffy as it might be now. My uncle Frank is a top-notch carpenter, and the rest of the crew followed directions well and worked hard. So by the end of the week, the cabin was basically done, minus a few finishing touches, like a metal roof, loft stairs, and exterior log sealer. Those came a little later on, but before winter took the UP by the throat. I don't recall having any major construction issues, although it was more than twenty-five years ago, so the details are a little fuzzy. The fact that it's still standing and working fine with very little maintenance is certainly a testament to the quality of the job our construction crew did and the fact that the plans must have been at least halfway decent.

In hindsight, there are a few things I might have done a little differently, but not much. Mainly, I would have used heavier-duty hinges on the doors to keep them from sagging. I swapped out to heavy-duty hinges several years ago. And I would have tried harder to find all windows that open. Only three of seven windows can be opened for ventilation, although the windows were all free, which I wouldn't change. The other thing I should have done differently is to complete all the finish work in a more timely manner instead of spreading it out over roughly twenty years. Once construction was complete and the cabin was useable, priorities and urgency changed. Regardless, we've been enjoying the cabin as a family retreat for about twenty-six years now, so it's all worked out fine, and I really can't complain. Though I'm prone to do it anyways now and then, most of my complaints are just about trying to keep the mice out. You would think that a trained engineer could outsmart a mouse.

About a month after everything was buttoned up for winter, I couldn't resist trying it out during the first week of firearm deer season, even though I suspected the hunting would actually be better at home in Jackson County. I slept on the wood floor with a thin sleeping pad from our camping equipment for three less-than-restful nights. Days were spent prowling the surrounding woods in search of antlered deer. I started out carefully and methodically still-hunting our eighty acres, but after the entire first day turned up not a single deer sighting, antlers or not, still-hunting transitioned to slow walking, which eventually morphed into somewhat slower-than-normal hiking.

After another day of not even seeing any deer tracks, I also decided to forego focusing on our property and freely wandered around all of the area's two-tracks just to see if anything was going on anywhere. In three days of pretty serious wandering, I crossed one set of tracks that were old enough to just vaguely resemble deer tracks. Sometime later, I found out that as soon as the snow starts collecting, every deer in the area heads south to the Tahquamenon River vicinity. Still, I got to know our new cabin along with the surrounding forest and trails, which started our long string of cabin adventures.

Relatively early on, Julie's dad and stepmom bought us a tandem stroller with bicycle tires so we could more easily cart the kids around on our hikes. It was comfortable enough that the girls could easily sleep if they needed to, so longer hikes through nap time weren't an issue. We soon found our way to an agate beach on Superior. There were a few places the old two-tracks crossed shallow creeks, which the twenty-inch bicycle tires handled just fine. In fact, the kids thought it was great fun crossing the creeks in their cart. To tell you the truth, so did I! Playing in moving water has been a favorite thing of mine most of my life, or at least all of it that I can remember. We never did find any true collectable agates, but it was enough agate material to keep us (okay, me) coming back pretty much every time we visited the cabin.

Late one afternoon, as Julie and I were saying we needed to get going back to the cabin, we pressed on a tiny bit farther west along the beach than usual. In the distance was the faint shape of a lighthouse tower showing above the trees. I guessed it was several miles away. It was too far for us that day, but with Julie being a lighthouse lover, we were destined to make it there soon.

We typically only made it to the cabin once a year, so "soon" turned into a couple of years by the time we found the trail that led to it. The lighthouse turned out to be Crisp Point. For the first few years, it was just the old light tower without many visitors. We still visit most every time we're at the cabin, although it's changed a lot, especially the number of people visiting. The biggest change, though, is that there's now seven of us in our group when we visit, as both of our girls are married and one has a young daughter of her own. I'm now pushing my granddaughter in that same three-wheel cart, and we still have fun fording small streams on the way. We still hunt for agates, and I'm still looking for "the big one." Fortunately, most of the adventure is in the searching.

Our string of adventures based from that eighty-acre plot of land in the middle of the woods now spans more than twenty-six years. They're all part of what we simply refer to as "the cabin."

It may be remote, but we have plenty of neighbors. Deer, squirrels, chipmunks, owls, sandhill cranes, bears, and moose are just the beginning of the list. We only actually saw a moose once, a young bull, trotting down the seasonal sand road in front of us as we drove out. At first glance, I wondered what a horse was doing out there, but then I noticed that the horse had small antlers. It was probably a fifteen-second encounter some twenty-five years ago, but I can still see him trotting down the middle of my mind's road.

Another time I was taking a short walk by myself and found fresh moose tracks crossing the road. About the time I saw the tracks, I heard something big crashing away through the brushy woods. I only caught a brief glimpse, but I'm pretty sure it was kind of my second cabin moose sighting.

Bears, on the other hand, we've had more than a couple of encounters with. During one of my cabin-building prep trips, I took my usual evening trail walk. Sounds of a rotted log being dismantled emanated from around a bend in the trail. Poking my head around the corner, I saw the big black north end of a bear facing south, digging for dinner about fifteen yards away. I quietly turned around and shortened my evening walk.

We've heard them indignantly woofing at us from the cover of thick brush and seen their tracks in the sandy roads and trails, and one afternoon, while working on chinking between the cabin logs, I had one come strolling down the trail twenty yards away. Once it noticed me, that encounter was quickly over. I had a camera nearby, but the picture only shows a blurry bear butt disappearing into some brush.

One afternoon during bear season, Julie was sitting in a rocking chair, reading on our porch. The not-too-distant baying of hounds told the story of a chase unfolding. Julie looked up to see a half-grown cub eyeing her from not more than ten yards away, looking intent on joining her on the porch. It apparently decided that hooking back up with mom, whom we assumed was leading the chase, was a better option and promptly disappeared into the woods.

One year, I adopted a bear hound named Suzy—for thirty minutes or so. We met on our trail through the property late in the afternoon. I was startled when she came trotting out of the deep ferns along the trail. She seemed elated to see me and didn't hesitate to follow me back to our cabin. I figured somebody would be looking for her, so I led her down toward the road—*road* meaning the main two-track through our property. As soon as I reached the road, a white pick-up with dog boxes in the back pulled up. The lady behind the wheel leaned out the window and asked if I had seen a stray bear hound. Before I could answer, the dog came trotting down our drive. The lady exclaimed "Suzy!" which was how I came to know her name. I thought I should point that out so nobody mistakenly assumes I'm a Doctor Doolittle prodigy or dog whisperer or something. Anyway, Suzy happily jumped into one of the boxes. The lady thanked me. Then she and Suzy headed off to rejoin the rest of the pack.

A few years ago, I was at the cabin by myself for a few days of projects. One of the projects was a hike out to Superior to look for agates. On the way out to the road in the morning, I found what looked like a recently deceased doe lying right along our drive. I was pretty sure it wasn't there when I drove in late the night before. After taking a suspicious look around, I continued on to the lake. When I returned in the evening, the deer was gone. It was too big for a couple of coyotes to move very far, and there were no signs of it being eaten or dragged, so I could only conclude that it was the doings of a bear—and a good-sized one at that. The woods took on a bit of a creepy feel, but I reminded myself that the bruin was probably off taking an after-dinner nap on the forest equivalent of a couch. Still, my senses were on high alert as I made my way to the cabin through the evening woods.

Just recently, we were at the cabin for our annual family fall gathering. Bear season was in full swing, so the distant sound of baying hounds wasn't uncommon. One morning, as the barking got close, we heard something that wasn't barking breaking branches as it ran through the woods. After the pursuing pack noisily passed by readily within sight, my granddaughter wanted to head over in that direction to take a look around. So she and I took a short stroll. As we stood there looking around in the woods, three more dogs came barking their way through. The first two ran by in the ferns about fifteen yards away, but the last one popped out into the trail we were on and headed down the trail straight at us. That prompted a loud scream from my granddaughter, which sent the hound running off into the woods. So I can only assume that facing a screaming four-year-old is apparently scarier than facing a mad bear.

I've never hunted much at the cabin since that first deer hunting attempt. The kids and I hunted small game once, but that was about it. I may consider bear hunting there (for obvious reasons), assuming I draw a tag at some point, but for the most part, the cabin is a place to relax and enjoy the simple life. It's a place for cooking over the fire, walks in the woods, tree climbing, exploring, and enjoying family time—things most people don't do much anymore and things that, unfortunately, many people have never done and probably never will. In some ways, it's a time machine transporting us back to a time before electricity and indoor plumbing, when oil lamps and a woodstove provided light and heat. There's a covered porch for rocking in wooden rockers, even when it's raining or snowing. Evenings are spent sitting in front of the open woodstove, talking, playing games, and enjoying plenty of good food. A little laughter isn't uncommon either.

Our driveway is a two-track that ends seventy or eighty yards shy of the cabin, so the modern world of automobiles isn't visible from our windows. Looking out the front windows, the scene is a fern-filled meadow surrounded by maples, dotted with blueberry bushes, and accented with pine and spruce. A couple of small west-side windows provide a view of our trail winding through the woods from the parking area. The back windows peer into the surrounding maple beech woods, where you can still see the old fort our girls built some fifteen years ago by leaning long, stout dead branches against a small trio of maples. They've added a few new branches now and then over the years, but every year, I'm amazed it's still standing.

Inside, the cabin is one open room with log steps ascending to an open loft that covers half of the room. It's definitely a family cabin, low on privacy, amenities, and maintenance but high on simple living and shared time close to nature, just the way a family cabin should be. As I mentioned earlier, we haven't quite figured out how to keep mice out, and after many years of trying, I'm not sure we ever will. So we just have to watch where and how we store our food, but our little "guests" do provide evening entertainment sometimes.

Many people we know have camps within thirty minutes or so of home, which isn't a bad idea because you would tend to use it more if it's convenient, although convenient places sometimes lose that feeling of being someplace special. Ours is a three-hour drive away, which, by UP standards, isn't all that far, but it's far enough that it still feels special when we go there. A lot of family memories live there. They stir around and give me glimpses into the past whenever I visit. Sometimes in the evening, when I'm there alone to work on projects, I'll sit by the old woodstove in my wooden rocking chair with a glass of wine and relive numerous episodes.

We're still actively building that collection of cabin memories, and God willing, hopefully we'll be able to continue our adventures there for years to come. As the world keeps rushing forward faster and faster, it's nice to still be able to take a slow step back now and then. I don't recall if that was part of the original dream or not, but it's certainly part of the reality of what we simply call *the cabin*. Or should I say camp?

PADDLING

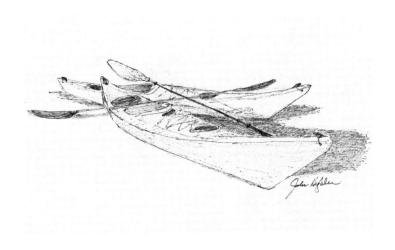

Paddling connects you to the water you're on. You become part of the lake, one of its features, like a colorful stone or brooding boulder strewn across the bottom, like a wave texturing its surface. Its mysteries begin to open as you peer closely into its depths. You become part of the lake's history, with each dip of the paddle propelling you deeper into its future.

Paddling past stately historic houses and summer cottages, Grand Island seemed pretty tame. I reminded myself that when you're paddling in Superior, tame can be a momentary thing. My wife, Julie, youngest daughter, Megan, and I were on our first real outing with our new kayaks, heading for the Murray Bay campground on the south end of Grand Island. I knew our eleven-foot Perception Sport boats weren't really meant for water like Superior, but we had tailored the trip around their limitations. We were only paddling for a couple of days, not going far from where we could get out of the

40

water if necessary, and we were staying away from areas too exposed to the open lake.

We headed east from the crossing to Williams Landing. The plan was to explore as far as the old East Channel lighthouse. After setting up camp at Loon Call, we took a paddling tour of Murray Bay with a lunch stop at Muskrat Point. Even though the town of Munising is visible across the end of Munising Bay, with plenty of wildlife and enough forest to honestly get lost in if you're not careful, Grand Island still has the feel of being on the edge of the wild. Leaving Muskrat Point, the rocky Grand Island shoreline begins to look and feel more like the untamed Superior shoreline the Ojibwa and early explorers knew before the heavy hand of civilization started leaving its mark on the land.

As we neared Wick Point, at the southern tip of the island, the sand and cobble shoreline transitioned to rock outcrops and large boulders. That was where I first noticed the scents of fresh water, sandy soil, and north woods trees mingling in the mild breeze. It was probably there all along. My mind was just preoccupied. Just around the point, we encountered a lone boulder the size of a large shed, just offshore, with a few small trees eking out a living on it. They looked a little ragged, but they were alive and still reaching for the sun. A good object lesson for us all, I thought.

Near the old East Channel light, a scattering of quiet cottages temporarily brought us back to present times in our man-made world, but the wild was still visible just up ahead. Reaching our lighthouse destination relatively early in the afternoon left plenty of remaining daylight to explore. While we were bobbing around, studying the weathered wooden structure, wondering what stories it held, my eyes and imagination kept straying to the decorated sandstone cliffs beginning to rise from Superior just past the lighthouse. The explorer in me just couldn't help wondering—or wandering. Julie and Megan laughed when I finally suggested we paddle a little farther. I'm sure they expected it and were probably surprised it took me so long to make the comment. Conditions were still looking good for safe paddling, so we cautiously paddled on, keeping track of time so we had a good idea of how long it would take us to get back to an area where we had access to land if the need arose.

For the next hour or so, we slowly paddled and explored a miniature Pictured Rocks Lakeshore. There were small caves, portals, sandstone formations, waterfalls, and seepages dripping from undercut bowls in the cliffs. We were able to paddle through one of the portals, and I sat for a minute with a small waterfall drumming on the nose of my kayak. It may sound like such an unspectacular thing to do, but if you've never had the opportunity before, it's like reaching out and touching a wild animal, but without the risk of getting bit.

We were almost to Trout Bay when the choppiness of the lake began increasing. It was getting close to 4:00 p.m., and we were coming into exposure to the open lake, so I decided it was time to turn the adventure south and head back toward camp. We maintained our relaxed exploration pace until we reached the lighthouse and summer cottages. That was when we could feel dinner calling, so we began paddling in earnest, looking forward to a hot meal and crackling campfire, just as any voyager would.

A couple of days later, Megan headed out from Munising with our oldest daughter, Amy, so that they could enjoy the last bit of our vacation together at Amy's house in Negaunee. We're thankful that they've always been close and still enjoy spending time together, so we had no objections to them heading out on their own for our last full day in the area. Julie and I toted our kayaks over to Miner's Beach, intent on spending time exploring the immediate area. Waves were a little more pronounced than I liked, but we still felt comfortable with them. We just limited the scope of our explorations a little more than originally planned.

First, we headed east past Elliot Falls, studying the small shoreline caves, colors, and formations close-up, like only a small shallow-draft craft can. That's one of the beauties of kayaks besides maneuverability; shallow water and barely submerged rocks don't pose much of an issue. This was our first reach-out-and-touch-them experience with the Pictured Rocks shoreline. To me, making an intimate connection like that is the way it's meant to be done.

We made it as far as the first couple of painted coves east of Miner's Beach before I decided it was time to turn around in order to maintain a safe distance to land access. Before we retreated, though, we had time to admire some of the artwork in the Pictured Rocks gallery as a bald eagle soared overhead, riding unseen currents along the cliffs. Red-orange iron, white calcium, blue-green copper, and black magnesium looked like finger-painted stripes down the sandstone wall.

After Julie took a potty break at Miner's Beach (the beach outhouse, actually), the waves were beginning to diminish. I had seen a photograph at a gift shop in town of some cool-looking caves and portals titled *Miner's Castle Portals*. Miner's Castle was only a couple hundred yards or so from the west end of the beach, so we had to go take a look. In the back of my mind, I half expected that the photographer had somehow enhanced the features beyond reality and that we were just going to find some blah-looking holes in the cliff. As we paddled around the base of Miner's Castle, I was glad to find that my suspicions were wrong. In fact, I found the picture didn't do reality justice. Not that there was anything wrong with the photograph. It was beautiful. But the picture primarily showed the outside of the caves and portals. As with most photographs, it couldn't possibly capture the feeling of paddling inside or through those features. There were only a few openings, but we spent at least forty-five minutes engrossed in them. That's the beauty of having your own kayaks and going on do-it-yourself trips. You're on your own schedule, and plans can easily change as opportunities arise.

I don't know how long I sat entranced in each cave, but I felt like it wasn't long enough. Sunlight was filtering in, illuminating the water with a blue-green glow. I had thought ahead to bring a headlamp, which intensified the banded colors. It felt like I was living a *National Geographic* story. Even after we decided we should pull out and head back to the beach, I was hesitant to leave, still trying to memorize every detail. Personal connections like that are hard to break away from.

As we paddled the short distance back to Miner's Beach, I told Julie that as far as I was concerned, the new kayaks had already paid for themselves.

That was all back before we moved north full-time. Now Superior is less than ten minutes away from our home in three different directions. Within fifteen minutes, I can be on four different rivers. Paddling opportunities are certainly not lacking here in the UP. Since making the move, we've added a couple of seventeen-foot sea kayaks to our fleet, which now includes five kayaks and two canoes. They all serve different purposes, and we use them all. I still have a couple of other boats on my wish list—an old wood and canvas canoe and a hand-built cedar-strip canoe—but I think they'll be on that list for a while. In some ways, that's fine. It gives me something else to dream about in addition to upcoming adventures. Dreams like that are part of what keeps me going through the ups and downs of day-to-day life.

One of the nearby rivers, the Laughing Whitefish completes its journey to Superior five minutes from our home. Like most good things close to home, we don't take advantage of the opportunity as often as we should or as often as I would like. There always seems to be something more pressing or something more pressing has left me not feeling much like venturing out again that day. One of the times we did venture out for a near-home paddling excursion was in early May, while there were still near-shore collections of icebergs decorating some of the sheltered Superior bays.

We launched our kayaks into an orange river in the early afternoon sunlight. Water was still swift and high from spring run-off, and there was still a tinge of chill lingering in the light breeze. A fine mist rolled across barren sand as it warmed in the sun. Friendly amber shallows of the river mouth sandbar abruptly dropped off to the dark unknown of Superior. A dense flow of pack ice guarded the bay 150 yards off shore, protecting mingling ducks, geese, and gulls. We paddled out to explore the edge of the ice flow and mingle with the ice. White, slushy tops of individual ice chunks gave way to smooth amber sculptures beneath the surface. Faceted crystal creations randomly jutted upward here and there toward the melting heat of the sun. Close up, the ice was constantly gurgling, dripping, creaking, and dropping pieces into the water. Bubbles rose from submerged forms in a constant stream as the ice was slowly giving way to spring. Slight undulations posing as waves were lulling the ice-pocked waterscape.

Bobbing with the ebb and flow, looking out over an artic scene, I felt like I should be watching for whales. Off the tip of Laughing Whitefish Point, striped red and gray sandstone bedrock was visible, extending out some two hundred yards from shore, pointing to the open lake.

Looking east, I could see the western cliffs of Grand Island. To the west, where the ice pack was slowly heading, I could see the hills rising above miniature Marquette. In between were a pair of bright kayaks peacefully bobbing with the pack, like a couple of multicol-ored icebergs caught up in the rhythms of spring.

More recently, we paddled through that same area in those same kayaks, but it wasn't the same. This time, it was late June. All traces of ice were gone, although you couldn't tell by the water temperature. Leaves were fully open, but newly opened maple leaves along the river mouth, yet to take on their summer chlorophyll mask of green, were still in varying shades of red, looking more like early autumn than early summer. They caught me by surprise, as did the realiza-tion that, in only about three months, these same maples would be in their early autumn attire, looking about the same, as the trees prepared for their winter rest. But this wasn't the time to be ponder-ing autumn. It was the time to be pondering a cool, bright summer Superior afternoon. So we turned or attention back to the flow car-rying us out into Superior.

Right where the river squeezed between sand dunes flanking each side, there seemed to be a current flowing in from Superior like a tide rolling in. I assumed it was the result of a seiche, which, in laymen's terms, is basically the lake sloshing around on a grand scale. On a local scale, it resembles an ocean tide. The battling cur-rents resulted in a swirl, causing sand to boil up from a deep hole being excavated in the river bottom. Our boats spun in the twirl-ing currents as I pondered the phenomenon at hand. As we paddled out of the swirl, amber-orange water gave way to beige on the river mouth sandbar, then to shades of blue out into the open lake. The cool breeze flowing in from Canada, causing a choppiness on the surface, felt refreshing after a few hours of lawn mowing earlier that afternoon. Refreshing is certainly one of the many traits of Superior!

I bobbed around, taking in the 360-degree view. The river mouth surroundings beyond nearby dunes were early-summer lush. To the west, beyond the nearby point marking the west edge of Michigan Nature Association property, were the hills above Marquette, with the Huron Mountains stretching north.

We paddled out a hundred yards or so from shore to a patch of red sandstone bedrock barely six inches below the surface, almost an island but not quite, causing mildly rolling waves to break into whitecaps. Sunlight glimmered in the changing water patterns. The surrounding blue was crystal clear as it slid across the rock formation. We paddled on another half a mile or so, mostly just enjoying being part of the lake.

On our way back into the river, we found that the battle of the currents was over. All that remained was the flow of the river gently rolling through a hole that marked the battleground. A choir of birds were singing summer songs, waves were gently kneading the sandy beach, and bugs were kept at bay by the light Canadian breeze. Lake and river were again at peace. As we passed between river mouth dunes, frogs were conversing as I eyed some deer tracks in the sand along the river. Yellow lily pad flowers preparing to open marked the entrance to a quiet backwater as we paddled by. It was all attractive and inviting, but my thoughts were still out in the lake, as they often are.

Superior certainly isn't lacking for paddling opportunities. Exploring the Presque Isle shoreline by kayak had been on my to-do list for over a year before everything lined up, and it finally became a reality. Everything lined up, meaning we finally had time and needed to go to Marquette for other things anyway when Superior was calm enough to readily paddle. Julie needed to pick up one of her paintings at Zero Degrees Gallery, and our sea kayaks were still on our Explorer from a storm-failed attempt at kayaking in AuTrain the previous evening. Superior is quite often calm—or at least calmer—in the morning, so we decided to get an early start. The lake gave us a couple of hour's window of decent paddling, and with it being a weekday right after fourth of July, we were the only explorers. That rocky shoreline, pocked with nooks and crannies and small caves, is a prime easy-to-get-to paddling destination, so I was surprised nobody else was there. We found some of the most spectacular and interesting views to be within sight of the Upper Harbor break wall.

I'm not a geologist, but places like Presque Isle and the islands up to Little Presque Isle make me want to study geology to better understand what I'm looking at. Then again, sometimes having mysteries to ponder keeps your imagination sharp. The most intriguing aspect of those formations to me is what I call spiderweb features in the rocks. There are entire cliffs with white quartz-based veins running all through them in intricate patterns and random wanderings. I've seen stones that fit the palm of my hand with numerous white strands winding through them, but I never realized that there were large cliffs just like that. I'm sure there are theories as to what caused this phenomenon, and digging into those details is on my list. I just haven't got that far down the list yet, but it gives me something else to look forward to. That's one of the things that keeps me going—having interesting things to look forward to and learn about. Anyway, I would be willing to bet that most people living in Marquette don't even know those features exist in that Superior shoreline just outside of town. Sadly, many may never know.

Seeing interesting geological features and other shoreline sights isn't the only benefit of paddling adventures. Paddling is more than a physical activity, more than mere exercise. It goes beyond simply interacting with water and shoreline.

The freedom of paddling, quietly skimming across the water's surface while peering into or pondering its benthic features, is addicting. Whether it's a lake, river, pond, or wooded flooding, in some ways, it doesn't really matter. You and the water are part of each other. There's a relationship.

I feel a relationship, to some degree, with every body of water I've ever paddled, from rushing torrents to tranquil backwaters. Like most types of relationships, those with water naturally form at differing levels. Over the years, I've found my relationship with Lake Superior is different than the others.

Superior pulls me in and wraps itself around my entire being. It always has, even when I was a kid. I don't know if it's because of the shear immensity, the incredible variation of colors, the clarity, mysterious rocky bottom, the wild shorelines, or the combination of all of it enveloping my senses. Superior grabs my imagination and my heart. So does paddling it. I've been blessed with opportunities to paddle numerous places across the Upper Peninsula, scenic lakes and rivers, as well as the Les Cheneaux Islands of Lake Huron and Garden Peninsula area of Lake Michigan, but I keep coming back to Superior.

One of the things I love about Superior is the range of colors it assumes. I've seen amber orange to beige, the entire range of blues and greys, black, white, and silver, just to name a few. Depending on location, time of day, season, and weather, Superior's hues could rival the color splotch selection of most paint stores. It embodies so many different moods—some telling, some deceiving—and those moods can change in minutes, leaving you in awe or in trouble. Its clarity grabs my mind and pulls it into its depths. Sometimes it magnifies bottom features. Other times, it softens them to the point of being surreal. It always plays with my imagination—sometimes intriguing, other times spooky—yet I can't help but stare, wanting more, looking for meaning. Answers are difficult to find. Questions are easy. I keep coming back, and I'm rarely disappointed unless, of course, I come without an open mind or with preconceived answers.

Paddling in Superior, I feel part of its immensity. I feel fluid, like part of the water. I feel freedom of mind, like a burden has been lifted and I should be thinking deep, flowing thoughts, but it's usually a relatively short stay and those thoughts remain just out of reach. Sometimes it feels like there is just too much to take in and ponder, and my mind just can't open up fast enough or big enough to hold it all.

Paddling, especially in Superior, invokes a sense of freedom, like being able to open your arms and soar through the air. On calm, glassy water, the line between reflection and reality disintegrates. Water and air become one and the same, making it difficult to distinguish which fluid you're paddling through. In a canoe or kayak, you can explore things only dreamed of from shore, unlocking mysteries or simply satisfying curiosities. You become part of the water, an active participant, rather than just a distant spectator. The physical course you've charted often doesn't matter. Your mind can paddle wherever the water takes it.

HITTING THE TRAILS

Sometimes a leisurely stroll is the quickest way
to get where you really need to be.

For me, serious hiking goes all the way back to when I was a kid of ten or twelve years old. My next-door neighbor Joe and I would often take hikes into the surrounding woods and fields with day packs our moms made for us. We had big outdoors adventures, even though we didn't cover large distances. I don't know about Joe, but I had big outdoors adventure dreams as well.

Family summer vacations included some minor hiking, but they were mostly camping outings. Then in high school, my parents gave me a frame pack for Christmas and allowed me to participate in a couple of out-of-state backpacking trips organized by our school, which seriously fanned the flames of my growing passion for backcountry travel and exploration. After I upgraded to a high-end frame pack, my dad and I ventured north for a few days to try it out in the Porcupine Mountains Wilderness State Park. He used my old K-Mart backpack, while I tested out my new Kelty pack. It felt like a Cadillac of a backpack. If I remember correctly, we were only out for three days and two nights, but it meant a lot to me to have my dad, who wasn't a backpacker or even a big hiker for that matter, to share the experience with. It was only my second serious backpacking trip, but I was the seasoned veteran of the group, so Dad let me take charge. I was sixteen, so Dad would have been thirty-nine. I knew the relatively small inexpensive pack was rough on him, but he never complained. In fact, in all of the time I spent outdoors with my dad, I don't ever recall hearing him complain. He just loved being outside, and he loved doing things with his family. He passed away only four years after that trip, but I carry a lot of good lessons from him, and I remind myself sometimes that I should try harder to live up to his examples, especially when it comes to complaining.

My wife, Julie, and I enjoyed lots of outdoors treks with our daughters when they were growing up. We started them out early, taking hikes from our cabin near Tahquamenon Falls when they were still young enough that I would push them in a three-wheeled cart with bicycle tires on it so that it could handle loose dirt and rough terrain. We have pictures of me pushing the girls in that cart through stream crossings, over downed trees, and through big mud puddles in the trails out to Lake Superior and later to Crisp Point Lighthouse. That was when the lighthouse was nothing more than an abandoned light tower on a lonely cobble beach. For the last few years, I've had the joy of pushing my granddaughter out to those same places in that same cart. Our first hike like that with her left me a little teary-eyed, but I'm getting to the point in my life where a lot of memories and special family activities seem to do that to me. Maybe I'm just getting soft and mushy as I age, but I prefer to think I'm taking lessons from my dad to heart.

When our youngest daughter, Megan, was five, we took a family backpacking trip along part of the Pictured Rocks National Lakeshore. Our route was from Miner's Castle east to Chapel Rock and back. We spent five days covering about twenty-five miles. Megan's "pack" was a fanny pack rigged up with suspenders to hold it up. She carried a few toys and a snack. Our oldest daughter, Amy, who was almost eight at the time, carried most of her own stuff in a large day pack. We were using two small two-person tents that Julie and I had acquired during our single years. The first night, I was so beat from carrying extra gear that I fell into a deep-sleep snoring session. In the other tent, Julie had to assure Amy that there wasn't a bear prowling around, growling, that it was just Dad snoring. Megan, who was sharing the tent with me, never mentioned it.

One of the trip highlights was when we were camping near Chapel Rock. After playing in the cascading falls at the creek mouth, the girls and I waded up the creek to get back to camp instead of walking the trail. They thought it was a great adventure. To be honest, so did I. Sometimes it doesn't take much to create a memorable event, just a little something out of the ordinary.

Now that we live not too far from the Pictured Rocks, we hike and explore there regularly. In fact, we recently finished covering pretty much all the trails in the Pictured Rocks trail system. That certainly doesn't mean we're done hiking there. For one thing, we have some favorite areas we like to revisit whenever we can, like the mature Red Pine forest near Twelve-Mile Beach Campground. The Chapel Rock area is another one of our favorites.

Late one afternoon in early May, we set out to hike the Chapel-Mosquito loop. We headed out the east side of Chapel Creek so we could see the falls. Our plan was to follow the lakeshore trail west from Chapel Rock and then follow the trail west of Mosquito River back to our vehicle so we could visit Mosquito Falls as well. It's a nice loop of about ten miles with plenty of interesting scenery and Superior views, including Lover's Leap.

About a mile or so before we reached Mosquito Campground, I noticed what looked like smoke not far ahead of us. My first thought was that we must be closer to the campground than I realized, but when we reached the source of the smoke, it turned out to be a hollow tree trunk about seven feet tall that was burning inside. How it had ignited, I have no idea because there hadn't been any recent lightning and there was nobody around. The reason notwithstanding, it was on fire. The inside of the hollow trunk was covered in glowing coals. Small flames danced here and there, and glowing pieces were dropping into the dry leaves around the stump where several spots were smoldering. In disbelief, I looked around again, and Julie and I were the only ones there. We only had about a quart and a half of water left in our bottles, and the nearest water supply was Superior, which was at the bottom of about a sixty-five-foot cliff. So it looked like the responsibility to put out the fire was on me.

After quickly running through a few possible courses of action in my head, I used our water to at least dowse the worst of the glowing embers down in the core of the trunk and stomped out all the smoldering areas in the leaves and duff. Then I scooped up several handfuls of loose sand from the trail and further smothered what was still slightly glowing down in the core. After making sure there were no more embers poised to drop into the leaves, Julie and I made a quick hike to the Mosquito Campground, where Julie looked for help while I refilled our two one-quart water bottles in Superior. There was only one person in the campground, and he was tired from a brutal day of backpacking, but he did lend us two more quart bottles. So Julie waited at the camp while I made three more quick hikes back and forth between the Mosquito Campground's lake access and the burning stump, carrying a gallon of water at a time. After dowsing it with roughly three and a half gallons of water, the fire appeared to be extinguished. I checked around with my hand for any remaining hot (or even warm) spots and didn't find any. There was no more smoke coming from the trunk either, so I decided that the job was done.

During one of my hikes back to the burning tree stump, I had passed an older oriental couple that I recalled seeing in the parking lot just as we left our vehicle. When I returned to the Mosquito Campground to return the borrowed water bottles and hook back up with Julie, I found her visiting with the water bottle owner and the couple I had passed on the trail. As it turned out, they were from Hong Kong and were visiting the area after attending NMU's graduation ceremonies with a relative. The woman spoke no English at all, and the man spoke very little broken English. They had caught up to us while Julie was taking pictures of Chapel Rock and recognized us from the parking lot. They had no map or any idea about where they were, so when we headed west along the shoreline trail toward Mosquito, they assumed that must be a way back to the parking lot and followed us, having no idea we were on roughly a ten-mile hike. We got them back to the parking lot at 9:50 p.m., just as it was getting dark. As a side note, I did follow up with the park service to have them check to make sure the stump didn't somehow reignite. It didn't.

We've hiked various Pictured Rocks trails since then, but thankfully, none of the hikes have been as exciting as that one, which is fine by me. I'm glad we were able to put out the fire and help our visiting friends find their car, but a little less drama would not have hurt my feelings.

The first time Julie and I visited Isle Royale was a July trip. We were geeked about being there but didn't really know what to expect. After our obligatory orientation presentation from park staff, the traditional race to Three-Mile Campground was on. It wasn't exactly what I had hoped for as a first impression of the island, but being young and in good condition, we at least managed to get there near the front of the pack to secure a decent campsite. That's about all I remember of our first day because it was just a foot race to camp. It sort of reminded me of running cross-country races in high school.

The second day mellowed into quiet backpacking but still not much in the way of serious wildlife encounters we were hoping for, just nice scenery.

The third day started as just another day of hauling our gear through the woods to our next campsite. Then we heard a couple of branches break about fifty yards off the trail. We instinctively stopped to watch and listen. The next (much closer) branch to break sounded like something of substantial size. That was when the thought finally hit me. Moose!

Neither of us had ever seen a moose out in the woods before, so we weren't exactly sure what to do. It sounded close, much closer than I expected for my first no-barriers moose encounter. I wasn't sure if we should just stand still and watch or shed our heavy packs just in case we needed to make a run for a nearby tree. Before I could decide, what looked like a dark draft horse with three-foot-wide antlers stepped into the trail about fifteen yards in front of us. He paused in the trail, slowly turned his head in our direction, which exaggerated his antler size, and gave us a look. I still remember seeing the whites of his eyes as he rolled them our way. He apparently wasn't as impressed with us as we were with him because, after a few-second glance, he looked back straight ahead and methodically lumbered off into the trees. As he did, a second slightly smaller bull took his place in the trail and followed suit. I don't remember taking pictures, but there were several on one of our rolls of slide film when we got them developed—mostly in focus or at least in focus enough to know we had a close visit with a couple of bull moose.

That was our first of many brushes with moose while hiking and exploring over the years. One of our most memorable was also on Isle Royale, but it was during September, when bulls are a little crazed because of the mating rut. During that peak time of the breeding season, bulls are wound up and looking to fight anything and anyone. Anything that moves or even catches their attention is a potential target.

Early one morning, we were lying in our tent, awake but not yet up and about, when we heard a bull grunt. We got to our knees and peeked out our back window just as the bull stepped into the trail leading to our campsite, stopped, and eyed our bright-orange two-person nylon tent. From only ten yards away, I knew it wouldn't take him long to reach us if the mood struck him. I nervously started an inventory of nearby trees and an exit plan that didn't include taking the time to unzip the door. Before I had to put my newly hatched plan into action, he turned, headed off fifty yards into the woods, and started shredding the place. It sounded like someone had the blade down on their bulldozer and was driving it through the thick woods. We scrambled out of our tent for a look, but all we could see was the tops of small trees flailing around as they were being thrashed. Before we could decide whether to sneak in for a better view or not, the commotion stopped. In the relative hush, I picked back up on my "climbable tree" inventory just in case. Fortunately, we didn't need to use it. We never saw or heard him again.

A few miles outside of Copper Harbor, where US 41 ends in a turnaround loop, there is a gravel road heading off toward the tip of the Keweenaw Peninsula. Back in my college days, it was a four-wheel-drive trail going off into the unknown. Being that I didn't have a four-wheel drive vehicle back then, that road and the land it accessed remained a mystery. I suppose I could have obtained a map of some kind and just hiked it, but because I had lots of destinations and adventures ranking higher on my list, it just never happened.

As I said, that trail is now a regular gravel road—at least for a few miles—and maps of the area are readily available for mountain bikes and ATVs, so Julie and I are now in the habit of exploring the area whenever we're in the neighborhood. Usually it's during our mid-May, celebrate spring, beat the bugs, get out and play before we have chickens to tend to for the summer, week-long trip. We often camp at Fort Wilkins State Park and roam the Keweenaw for a week, which always includes at least a day of hiking one of the many roads/trails traversing the tip of the peninsula.

More often than not, our explorations near the end of the road revolve around agate hunting or at least reaching a new stretch of shoreline where I might do some agate hunting if I were so inclined. (Don't ask Julie about that.) One time, though, we meandered off around the south side of Lake Fanny Hooe to explore some of the newer biking/hiking trails. We were familiar with the general area from cross-country skiing adventures years ago. One of our goals was to hike the old trail we used to ski on just for the nostalgia of it. Our favorite old trail followed the edge of Lake Fanny Hooe for most of the distance of the lake before it climbed up into the woods and off toward destinations southward. The new trail, which is the only one showing on any maps, stays high in the woods, giving better overall views across the lake, but it lacks the personal contact with the lake that we always appreciated and wanted to reconnect with.

We didn't start until later afternoon, so we were running short on time by the time we neared the east end of Fanny Hooe. By that point, we had given up looking for our old trail and were just enjoying a stroll through the woods, periodically taking pictures of the views across the lake.

Just before it was time to turn around and head back, we passed through a slight opening in the forest. As we did, I nonchalantly glanced up the parting line through the trees, and a flashback hit me. Taking a couple of steps backward to realign with the opening, I found myself looking up the trail that was no longer there. Looking in the opposite direction, even without the bare dirt trail, I could plainly see the pathway through the trees angling down toward the lake.

Julie came back to see what I was up to. I pointed through the trees, and she immediately recognized the old trail too. We wanted to follow it back along the lake, but daylight was beginning to fade, and we weren't sure how difficult it would be to follow, so we just walked in the past for a hundred yards or so, then returned to the present and followed the new trail back out. We agreed we would come back some time to reminisce the full length of the lake. We haven't done it yet, but we will. Sometime.

That's one of the great things about hiking. You don't always have to make big plans in order to do it. You can make big plans if you want to, but it's not required. It requires so little gear and no special, high-end equipment. Typically, a pair of hiking shoes or boots and sometimes a small day pack gets you on the trail. In fact, special hiking shoes aren't even a requirement. When I was younger, I often just hiked in running shoes. I wouldn't suggest trading hiking shoes for sandals or flip-flops, as I've seen some people do, not unless you're trying to ruin your feet.

Hiking gets you in touch with the wild in a relatively low-key way. Options are extensive and can easily be adjusted to match anyone's distance ability. It's one of the most basic things a person can do and one of the best ways to get in or stay in shape for more major endeavors.

I often intermix comments about hiking, backpacking, and exploring all in the same discussion, even though there are some differences. In my vocabulary, hiking is just walking on the wild side, typically on a trail. Of course, that begs the question, if you're on dirt roads or two-tracks, is it still hiking or just walking? I guess it's the surroundings that matter, not what's underfoot, so instead of splitting hairs, we'll just call it all hiking. Backpacking is basically just extending hiking to a multiday event with camping in between. When we're traveling off trail, I usually refer to it as exploring. Not that any of that really matters. It's just the terminology I use. The important thing is to get outside, quietly travel under your own power, see the sights, and experience our natural world.

There's no telling how many miles I've covered hiking, backpacking, and exploring, even just since moving up to the UP, but I'm guessing it's a pretty hefty number. Hopefully, I've got a lot more years of foot travel in me. If I have any real say in the matter, I'll stop hitting the trails when they close the lid on me. Until then, I'm an adventurer looking for an adventure, and there's always a new adventure out there just waiting for an adventurer.

CAMPING

Campfires are time-machines. Stare into the flames of a campfire and you can visit every campfire you've ever had. Time and place don't matter. You're there. People and times long gone come to visit. Sometimes you find yourself gazing into a fire you didn't even know you remembered. Funny how those dancing flames penetrate our being and cut across the years. Then, quickly as you left, you return, with today's flames flickering in your eyes once again, looking forward to the next journey.

My camping experience goes back farther than I can actually remember. Old black-and-white photographs provide snippets of those memories that have somehow been lost to time. Family summer camping took us all over the state. Anywhere "up north" set my dreams in motion, but crossing "the bridge" was monumental. Even tourist attractions like Castle Rock, just outside of St. Ignace, were pure adventure in my young subdivision-raised mind. Places like Tahquamenon Falls, Pictured Rocks, Fort Wilkins, and Porcupine Mountains were nearly mystical.

My earliest camping memories are of a canvas tent roughly ten feet square back in the late 1960s or early 70s. Summer vacations and the smell of canvas go hand-in-hand in my mind. Whenever I catch a whiff of old canvas, I'm back in those carefree days again. I still have an old nylon tent that dates back at least forty years. It's not quite the same smell as canvas, but it's close enough. Last fall, when we unrolled that old nylon tent, I closed my eyes for a few seconds as a flood of memories poured out of it. That old-tent smell to me is camping. It's not the same in a fancy new trailer. It's like a comfy, faded pair of jeans compared to a new pair of dress pants. They both provide covering and pockets, but the faded jeans have history and character. Tents provide just enough shelter to protect you from the elements and biting insects while still keeping the feel of being out-side. Besides, rain on an old tent is more soothing than rain hitting a metal or plastic trailer roof. But I do have to admit that a trailer probably keeps the rain *out* better than an old tent.

It's not that you can't have adventures with a trailer. I remember our family camping at Fort Wilkins State Park after Mom decided we needed to "move up" to a pop-up camper. It was a fancy Apache hard-side camper. We were in a campsite on the east end of the east campground loop, right by the woods. Mom was lying awake in the early morning, listening to a chipmunk messing with a plastic dish-pan she had left out on the picnic table. The noise stopped for a minute, then started back up again, this time louder. Mom decided to get up and shoo the little critter away. When she popped open the camper door, she was startled to find herself only a foot away from the tail end of a large black bear that was trying to dig our plastic cooler out from under the camper. The door didn't stay open long, and she soon wasn't the only one awake.

Still, to me, camping involves a tent. There was a time when I felt that sleeping on the ground using only a thin pad under your sleeping bag was a necessary part of camping too. As I get older, though, I'm becoming less of a stickler on that one. I've used a cot a few times, even though we don't actually own any, and I have to admit that they're pretty comfy. I'm not sure if I'm ready to make the move to a cot of my own yet. It's partly because they're bulky and partly because we still do a lot of backcountry camping where you can't realistically use one, so why get spoiled? I have been enviously eyeing one of those cushy self-inflating sleeping pads that combine foam and air, but for now, the price tag is holding me at bay.

The first year we owned our Upper Peninsula property near Tahquamenon Falls, we spent a couple of nights camping there in the forty-year-old tent I mentioned earlier. Of course, at that point, it was twenty-seven years younger, and I don't recall it having that old-tent smell. But my memory is also twenty-seven years older now, so maybe the recollection of the tent smell and the event just got separated somewhere along the line.

We were too excited about owning property up north to wait until we could build a cabin—or at least I was—so we packed up our young family and our camping gear and headed north in late September of 1993. The property was mostly woods, which didn't accommodate a twelve-foot-square tent very well, so we set it up in the middle of the two-track that dead-ends on the property. It ended up being colder than expected, complete with a couple of inches of snow. Our youngest daughter was six months old, so she was fine as long as we kept her warm, fed, and in clean diapers. Our oldest daughter was three years old. As long as she had toys to play with and read stories before bed, she was fine with the situation too.

Julie and I were a little concerned, though, because we had a difficult time keeping the kids bundled up good all night. So we slept like worried parents, but the kids didn't seem to have any issues. Still, we decided to cut the camping a little shorter than originally planned. I still think about that camping experience every time we visit the cabin and walk past that spot on our two-track. Every now and then, when we're camping somewhere in that tent and I'm just lying there relaxing before I fade off into sleep, I'll take in a deep breath of that old-tent smell, and my mind will wander back there again. Funny how such a relatively minor experience can become so entrenched in your brain. But it's not a bad memory to have entrenched in my head. It always makes me smile when it bubbles to the surface, so I'm guessing it must be entrenched in my heart as well.

We now have a much newer dome tent that's smaller and lighter, but unless we're backcountry camping, where bulk and weight matter, I prefer the older big tent. Part of my bias might be the fact that you can stand straight up in the old tent and still have room to move around to get dressed. There's also plenty of room for whatever gear you want to bring in with you, without cramping your sleeping space. Then again, maybe it's just a nostalgia thing because I've noticed I'm getting more sentimental as I age. I suspect it's probably a combination of those things and maybe even a few other factors that I'm not even cognoscente of. The reason doesn't really matter anyway. I like the old tent.

We've been using it for our mid-May camping trip we got into the habit of going on in recent years. Typically, we use that time to camp at Fort Wilkins State Park near Copper Harbor so we can readily explore the northern reaches of the Keweenaw. The main bathroom and shower facilities usually aren't open at that time, but probably in big part because of that, we usually own the place. In the east side of the campground where we like to camp, it's not uncommon to have only a couple of other sites occupied besides ours. There have even been a few days where we were literally the only ones there. We have our favorite campsite, but I won't mention it here so as not to invite competition.

While we're there, we like to hike the trails and prowl beaches for agates. Before settling in for our evening campfire, we often take a long walk around the entire park, including the old fort. Quietly roaming around the fort as evening is setting in, it's easy to imagine a wilder Keweenaw and what used to be.

Sometimes it's difficult to decide where to take our evening walk because the same time we enjoy hanging around the fort and walking the Fanny Hooe lakeside trail, when the sun is getting low in the western sky, is also one of the best times to be beachcombing for agates. Walking Superior beaches toward the descending sun—or ascending in the morning—you'll see those opaque agates shining like miniature light bulbs compared to other beach stones. During that first and last thirty minutes of sunlight, I have a mental struggle trying to walk slow enough to catch details when I want to speed up to cover more ground before I lose the advantage of low-angle light. When it gets dark enough that all the rocks begin to look the same, it's time to work our way back to camp. It's campfire time.

For me, camping isn't camping without a campfire. Whether you use it for cooking, chasing off the evening chill, telling stories, or just listening to crackling flames while your mind wanders, a campfire is a camping necessity. Even when you're sitting in a crowded campground full of RVs and trailers, a campfire still evokes feelings of adventures in wild places. Somehow those dancing flames blot out present surroundings as they pull you in. Even when we're not camping, whenever I catch a whiff of wood smoke, I end up by a campfire somewhere in my mind.

The first time in recent years that we camped at Fort Wilkins in August, so Julie could participate in an art show in Eagle Harbor, we about went into shock as we pulled in. Our quiet little park had the look and feel of a small city, complete with high-rise camper buildings. It certainly wasn't our idea of peaceful camping, but once we convinced ourselves that we were only there for a place to sleep so we could have a booth at the art show, we managed to relax enough to start setting up camp. As I started pulling out tent poles, though, a sickening thought hit me. A few years earlier, a severe thunderstorm out in Glacier National Park had leveled our tent in the middle of the night and broke one of the main roof support poles. I managed to repair the pole, but it no longer folded up as short as the rest. It doesn't fit in the bag with the rest of the poles anymore, so we store it out in our garage, even though the rest of our camping gear is in our basement. As I was pulling out the poles, I realized the repaired pole was still in our garage, three hours away.

We ended up setting up the tent using a rope stretched between two trees in place of the missing pole. It worked okay, but one side of the roof had a little bit of a sag I just couldn't get out. That night, as we lay in our sleeping bags, listening to thunder sounding closer with each rumble, I started wondering how our jimmy-rigged tent would hold up. As usual, gusty winds led the way as the storm front moved in. The rain came in with a lackluster start but soon turned to what sounded like a power-washer spraying on the tent. Technically, the tent held up fine, meaning it didn't collapse on us like it did out in Glacier. It just didn't keep the water out. Our slightly saggy roof turned into a nylon bucket with a steady stream seeping through the bottom and recollecting in a puddle on the floor. The bigger the roof bulge got, the more the roof sagged, allowing the bulge to grow more. I ended up having to intervene every few minutes to empty the bulge. Otherwise, not only would the puddle on the floor have overtaken our sleeping bags, the tent's ability to continue holding up would have been in question.

The deluge went on for an eternal thirty minutes. After my final dumping of our roof, I got back in my sleeping bag, damp, chilled, and muttering things about our tent. The next day, I did admit that if "someone" had remembered to bring all the tent poles, it would've been fine. Now I can see it all as just part of the adventure of camping. That night, I somehow missed it.

More recently, we used that old tent for a week-long September stay in the Pictured Rocks National Lakeshore. To start out, we spent a couple of nights at the Twelve-Mile Beach Campground. Even though we've lived in the area for a few years, we had never camped in any of the main campgrounds. Part of the reason may just be that it's always seemed strange to me to camp only an hour or so from home. For Pictured Rocks, we usually just take day trips. This time, though, we wanted to be there to catch sunrises and sunsets on Superior without having to rush over there or rush home. Being able to settle in to a campfire after sunset sounded appealing too. We liked the feel of Twelve-Mile Beach being in the middle of a mature red pine forest, so that was our starting point.

We arrived late on a gloomy Sunday afternoon. After setting up camp at site number 19, we didn't have a lot of daylight left to work with, so we decided to just take a short trail hike over to Sullivan's Creek because we had never hiked that section of trail before. So why not start out with something new? For the return, we headed out to Superior because we didn't want to spend sunset hidden in the woods. About 7:30 p.m., the sun finally broke below the cloud cover, igniting the bottoms of the clouds. Beach rocks were glowing molten gold. Waves were building, curling white, before breaking across sand and cobble as the sun settled toward the horizon. Every few waves advanced the curving waterline a step more up the beach.

That night, our campfire wasn't anything memorable, but somewhere down the line, maybe I'll find myself staring into it again sometime.

Next day, we explored from Sullivan's Creek to Hurricane River mouth, first by Superior shoreline, then returning by trail. An interesting collection of lakeside boulders kept us busy for a while. I didn't keep track of exactly how long because we weren't on the clock. We often get caught up in looking at lakeside rocks, regardless of size. With the astonishing variety of colors and patterns, I can't help but to wonder how so many people can simply brush it off as happenstance. I see it as purposeful artwork on a grand scale, created by a grand artist.

Misty morning gloom transformed to afternoon sun and sparkling whitecaps advancing on the beach. Over the course of a quarter mile, we passed four lone Canada geese. None appeared to be injured, yet they seemed unwilling to fly in order to get away from us. Each of them just cautiously eyed us as we carefully gave them room and passed by, leaving them to their business.

Numerous seeps run across the beach in that area, creating braided paths in the sand like hair flowing in a swirling breeze. The gentle flows created sand art in colors of black, red brown, and tan, exposing occasional colorful stones and incorporating them into the picture.

Just west of Hurricane River, I found myself marveling again. This time, it was wood—an old broken white pine that had succumbed to Superior poundings, bark cleanly removed by sandy waves and harsh elements, exposing swirls of grain in exotic patterns. Maybe I'm strange, but I have a thing for wood. Julie took some pictures with her ever-present camera, but pictures just don't even come close to doing it justice, which is typical, probably because pictures don't capture the surroundings or the experience. Still, we capture them as reminders.

Several times over those two days at Twelve-Mile Beach, I looked up and down the shoreline to find that we were the only souls on the beach. We were back out at the water's edge for sunset, with shades of amber and orange illuminating the scant collection of clouds, and once again, we were the only witnesses of the unfolding miracle. We soaked in the cool breeze and warm colors, feeling like we were the only ones in the world.

After those first couple of days, we moved camp over to Hurricane River Campground, partially because we wanted to move our exploring focus farther east and partially because I wanted to chase Hurricane River trout. We started with a three-quarter mile stroll out to AuSable Point Lighthouse. Four-foot waves were rolling in, holding a fifty-yard-wide band of tannin-leaden water from the river against the shoreline. Beyond was a hundred yards of aquamarine green-blue water, followed by dark blue to the horizon. Whitecaps highlighted the entire scene. The waves were coming from two different directions, colliding and merging into one. Afternoon sunshine made Superior seem perky.

Grand Sable Dunes to the east were bathed in sunshine, looking like a desert dropping into Superior waters—barren falling into abundance. A bank of puffy clouds mimicked the dunes below them, coming to a point near the horizon, where they abruptly ended.

Following the shoreline back toward camp, we found ourselves pondering the remains of an old shipwreck lying exposed on the wave-tattered beach—water-logged wood and rusted iron slowly losing their battle with the elements. Sunlight somehow seemed to bring hope to this past tragedy.

Back at Hurricane River, I lingered on a high bank overlooking a cascading waterfall not far upstream from the mouth, watching a few large fish swirling in and out of sight at the base of the falls. Three times, I saw a fish attempt the falls, a black silhouette against white foaming water. Only one made it to the top. A fisherman from Negaunee stepped in with a fly rod and orange yarn to simulate eggs from salmon coming to spawn. Over the course of thirty minutes, he caught a nice steelhead and a small coho. I thought of my own fly rod back at camp, as two more fish made a failed attempt at the falls, but it was nearly dark. Tomorrow, I thought.

The next morning, I was standing in the edge of the river, fly rod in hand, trying to simulate the results I had witnessed the previous evening. Over the course of about an hour, I successfully hooked two logs, but that was it. I began suspecting there were no longer any fish in the plunge pool, so I decided to put fishing on hold.

Kayaking was on our to-do list, but Superior was a little too agitated by our standards. Instead we ventured over to Grand Sable Lake. We had often eyed it while passing by on drives to Grand Marais but had never explored it by boat. Fall colors were still a little lacking around the lake, but having the entire lake to ourselves made for great exploring. Well, I guess I can't really say we had the lake to ourselves. Lots of ducks were there, as well as a pair of swans at the far end near the main feeder creek. A bald eagle eyed us from above as we watched a fisher snooping around the shoreline forest. Two small creeks cascaded into the lake, gurgling and singing. They were hidden in the trees, but their music gave them away.

Evening found me back in the Hurricane River—same place, same fly, same results as that morning. Again, I saw no sign of any fish. Obviously, I needed to rethink things over a campfire.

On the river, tunnel vision seemed to have had me in its grip. Sitting in the dark, staring into flickering flames, I couldn't see the tunnel, so trying something different clearly made sense. Flames always seem to burn through to simplicity.

The next morning was cold and rainy. Before we planned this camping trip, I had agreed to make presentations at the Conservation District–sponsored Agri-Palooza for area fifth graders. So I had to blow off fishing in order to fulfill my commitment. I would be making presentations about trout conservation on behalf of the local Trout Unlimited chapter, which I thought was pretty ironic being that I had to skip trout fishing to do it. Julie occupied herself around the campground area while I drove into town for part of the day.

I returned by midafternoon, wet from the waist down from constant rain running off my rain jacket. Rain stopped about the time I arrived back at camp. Julie and I decided to take a dry-out walk back out to the lighthouse. With wet pants (especially on the seat), wet long johns, and a wet bandana in my back pocket, it felt like I was wearing a soggy diaper for most of our walk. By the time we made it back to camp, I had mostly dried out. I was dry enough at least to put on my waders and give that fishing hole another shot. This time, I tied on a streamer. Forget what the other guy was having success with. It wasn't working for me.

Within thirty minutes, I had hooked six fish—four for just a few seconds and one long enough for a minor tussle until it did a tail walk across the water and threw my hook. I also had a twenty-incher chase my fly out onto the sandbar I was standing on before it turned and disappeared back into tannin darkness. The final fish—a small steelhead—put up a good fight but finally came to the net. As I went to remove the hook, it made one last violent shake, breaking off my tippet right at the fly, and promptly disappeared back into the hole.

Another half hour of diligent fishing produced nothing. Still, it had been a good evening of fishing, so I reeled in and headed back to camp, stopping for a quick look at the logjam just downstream from where I was fishing. From my vantage point on the high bank, I could see a few nice fish milling around in an unfishable area. As I was thinking that this might be where the fish from the hole above are probably disappearing to once they get a little spooked, out swam the small steelhead sporting my recently lost fly. I headed back to our last evening fire, enlightened.

The next morning, I made a quick check and found the fish all hanging out in the logjam instead of the falls plunge pool. After looking things over for a few minutes, I decided to leave on a good note, so we packed up our old tent and other gear and headed for home with plans for a long hike near Kingston Lake on the way to wrap up our week.

Having such a long history with camping like I do, it's one of those things that's so ingrained in me that it's part of who I am. Going forward, a few minor equipment tweaks may be in order, though. With the distance between me and sixty getting pretty short, I can see a little plusher sleeping pad in my future for backcountry camping. For car camping in state and national parks, I could even see myself in a cot. Maybe. If we find a good enough sale. As for accommodations, though, I don't see us making the move to a camping trailer. To me, camping still involves a tent.

IT'S A TWO-WAY TRAIL

You don't always need to go new places to see new things. Just look at old places with new eyes and appreciate where you are.

I was roaming our yard one late April evening, not necessarily doing anything in particular, just checking around to see how spring was progressing. Looking out our home windows gives a good view of what's going on, but the details are missing. Besides missing sounds and smells of the outside world, close-up details don't come into focus through a window. The first fern frons of the season and trout lily leaves just poking through the matted carpet of last year's leaves require more of an in-person view.

The slight breeze that just a couple of days before delivered a chill now had that lukewarm feel of having crossed the invisible line between winter and spring. It rippled the snowmelt puddles with the promise that winter was finally letting go. Mingled with this whispering breeze, there was another soft, barely audible sound. I couldn't quite make out the notes, but I knew the song. Canada geese were moving north. My eyes searched the southern sky, looking for that familiar V pointing north.

Standing there in the yard, I was sitting on my couch thirty-five years ago and some five hundred miles south, listening through an open apartment window to the conversations of the night. Some were faint and steady, passing by somewhere in the night sky. Others were loudly debating nesting sites along the swampy river out back. Many nights I sat there with the evening cool in my face, listening.

Aldo Leopold wrote of goose music too. He said, "If...we can live without goose music, we may as well do away with stars or sunsets." The music faded north as the faint check mark disappeared behind a screen of nearby trees. I hadn't been looking for anything particular beyond normal yard life, but something much bigger and wilder had reached out and touched me, leaving me to ponder bigger and wilder thoughts. That's how it works sometimes, especially here in the UP. You're not really looking for the wild, but it reaches out and touches you anyway, even in your backyard.

This past spring, I was watching a pair of Sandhill Cranes probing our backyard soil with their long beaks, searching for whatever it is that they're often searching for. Being April, it was that time of year when it's not uncommon to see turkeys using our open back yard as a courting ground as well. As the cranes were aerating our soil, a tom turkey emerged from our woods and headed straight over to join the cranes. The stubby beard sticking almost straight out from his chest told me he was a youngster, likely in his first courting season. As soon as he got near the cranes, he fanned his tail and began strutting around, putting on what I thought was an impressive show. I wasn't sure if he was confused by a rush of hormones and was seriously trying to attract the female crane away from what he thought was his competition or if he was just practicing so he'd be ready should he find himself in a real courting situation sometime. Either way, the female crane appeared unimpressed and disinterested. The male, however, was obviously annoyed by the show, regardless of its intent, and promptly chased the tom away before his lady had a chance to change her mind. The young tom wisely took it as his cue to move on.

I was looking out our back windows another late-April evening and spotted a pair of ruffed grouse in the northeast corner of our backyard. I tend to call them partridge, but I'm told that's a down-state term. Wanting to be considered a local, not just a transplanted troll (people living below the bridge), I now earnestly try to remember to call them grouse. Anyways, I quickly dug out my binoculars for a closer look. I really should keep them handy, being surrounded by woods like our house is, but I usually don't. I tend to like things to be put away where they belong. So when something interesting shows up in our yard, it's a scramble. You would think I'd learn, but I haven't. At least not yet.

The birds turned out to be males, and they were squaring off, periodically fluttering into the air a foot or so and raking their feet at each other. I assumed it was a territorial squabble of some sort. After a few minutes of watching through my binoculars, I left them be to go on about my business, which was probably something important, but I can't recall exactly what it was. Checking back now and then, I found the confrontation went on for at least thirty minutes, and I don't know how long they were at it before I noticed them.

The incident brought to mind the lone grouse I had seen a few days earlier, perched in one of our small apple trees just across the backyard, eating the swelling buds from the tree. That one I believe was a female, although I didn't get a close look because my binoculars were safely and properly tucked away in their case downstairs in my office. She spent quite a while helping herself to the buds to the point where I considered going out and running her off for fear of damage to the tree and a diminished apple crop, but then I reminded myself of the several years that tree had been there unprotected by me, and it was still doing fine. So I left her alone and just enjoyed watching life in action. (As a side note, the apple crop turned out fine.)

The first frog songs of spring always catch me by surprise. I usually begin listening for them too early in the season, and after a few days of no rewarding chorus, I tend to forget about it, my mind moving on to the myriad of other springtime thoughts. Then when I finally do hear it, I wonder if it really did just begin or if I've only been too preoccupied to notice until now. Every year, I come to the same conclusion that it really doesn't matter exactly when it started. I'm not collecting scientific data on frogs, so the important thing is to simply enjoy it when you hear it because, in the not-too-distant future, I'll be equally surprised when one day I realize that the performance is over and the voices that once emanated from every ephemeral pool in the woods are silent. Another season has slipped by in the neighborhood wilds.

One day in early May, I was relaxing in our four-season room when I heard the loud tapping of a woodpecker. Looking out the window, I spotted a northern flicker clinging to the front of one of our bluebird houses mounted on a tree about twelve feet from the house. He would spend a minute or two studying the small entrance hole. Then he would pound away at the birdhouse front, right next to the hole. The staccato sound from repeated attacks on that empty birdhouse resonated through our yard and our house, even when there were no windows open. About fifteen minutes later, he moved over to another of our birdhouses and continued pounding. At first, I thought he was attempting to enlarge the entrance hole, which I have seen done before but usually by pileated woodpeckers. Thinking about it a bit more, though, I concluded that he just liked the sound it made, and maybe he thought the local feathered ladies liked it too. I didn't need binoculars for that show. I just stood there and watched the free woods concert. I had witnessed similar concerts performed with dead trees, but that was the first time I had stage seating.

One morning in late May, I went out to resume garden preparation work where I had left off the previous evening. As I approached the garden, I noticed a big divot in the rototilled soil.

I thought, *Great. I haven't even planted yet, and something is already digging holes in our garden.*

Getting closer, I saw that the divot was actually part of a string of divots that stretched from one side of the garden to the other. Even closer inspection revealed that the bottom of each hole was pretty well packed down, other than a little loose dirt that had fallen in from the edges. As I stood there studying the marks, I finally came to the surprised realization that I was looking at moose tracks. At first, I was excited to think we had moose, or at least *a* moose in the neighborhood. Then I started wondering how in the world you protect your garden from a moose. I did a little checking around and found that, sometime during the night or early morning, our visitor had entered our yard through the west side trail, walked through the garden, exited twenty feet from the house, then veered around the house, and left by way of the east side trail. Had we been looking out any of our back windows, we would have been startled by the closest wild moose encounter we've ever had.

I later found out from neighbors down the road that a lone bull had been spotted in the area more than once. In fact, a friend that has a camp a few miles to the south said he had trail camera pictures of two different bulls. We saw muddy tracks along our side road one time since the garden visit, but that was it. Still, knowing they're out there is enough to keep me excitedly looking forward to a possible encounter one of these days. I think of it sometimes when I am slowly still-hunting through our woods, looking for deer. Just maybe...

Going out to feed the chickens isn't usually something that comes to mind when you think about encounters with the wild, but then again, neither is going out to tinker in the garden. Several times I have opened our chicken coop door and had a garter snake drop out from between the edge of the door and the frame. They're typically within a few feet of the ground, but one time, I had one surprise me from above eye level. Now I don't mind snakes. We see them regularly around our yard. And I know they keep insects and mice in check, but I'm not real fond of the idea of one dropping on me when I pull open a door. It hasn't actually happened yet, but it's been close.

At least those snake encounters were out in the chicken coop. We've run into garter snakes more than once in our living room too. How exactly they get in is still a mystery, but it's one I'd really like to solve. I think about it sometimes when I need to get up in the middle of the night for a nature call. As I get out of bed, I can't help wondering if I'm going to step on some squirming nature with my bare feet. Compared to that, I guess I'd rather find them in with the chickens.

Snakes are not the only wild encounters we have in the chicken coop either. For some reason, it tends to attract wolf spiders. I'm talking about those big dark hairy spiders with a body that's a good half inch in diameter or more. Including their beefy legs, they easily measure two inches or more across, and you can readily see their eyes. They look like a small tarantula to me. The first time I saw one in the coop was when our chicks were only a few days old. I recounted the chicks twice to make sure they were all still there. Those spiders give my wife, Julie, the creeps. So I'm always sure to mention to her when I see one—it's just a guy thing. One time when I saw one, I told her that I tried to catch it, but it lifted up the edge of one of the straw bales and ran underneath. She didn't laugh. It's just another part of living in the wild UP.

My most fun wild encounter at the chicken coop, though, was with a bear. It wasn't a close encounter, but considering how fast a bear can run, if you get a good look at one, it's a close enough encounter. In this case, it was early June, and I was on my way out for the last evening feeding. When I looked around, I noticed a large black animal moving through the woods just beyond the edge of our side yard. It was at a distance of fifty or sixty yards, which a bear can cover in just a few seconds. I wasn't sure if the bear saw me or not. It just kept walking parallel with the edge of the yard and disappeared into a thicker section of woods. I immediately snuck over to investigate just because that's the type of thing that I do but never saw it again. There was no noise from it crashing through the underbrush, so it must have just casually gone on about its business. With a smile on my face, I did the same.

I'm often figuratively touched by the wild UP, but I do recall being touched physically one time as well. I was wandering our yard, checking out flowers, not expecting any wild encounters except for maybe an occasional bee. Early in the tour, I was standing in front of our house, only a few feet from one corner, admiring some daylilies. Suddenly, a robin came flying around the corner of the house and flew right into the side of my head. I caught a quick glimpse out of the corner of my eye as the bird noticed me at the last second and tried to flare off to one side. It didn't hit me hard, but it was still hard enough to knock my hat off. It happened so fast that neither one of us even had a chance to make a sound—other than a slight thud. The robin flew away, apparently unscathed. I picked up my hat and chuckled. What else could I do?

That incident reminds me of another bird encounter. Being a little follicle-deficient on top, I tend to wear a bandana on my head to protect me from the sun when I work outside, especially in the summer when it's too warm for even a light hat. So I was out working in our yard with a red bandana on my head. When I stood still for a few minutes to survey the yard for the next possible project, a male hummingbird zipped in and hovered only a couple of inches from my forehead. I assumed he was thinking he had just found the mother of all flowers. It didn't take him long to realize his mistake—or the bird equivalent of that—and he moved on, looking for the real deal.

Late one August evening, my wife, Julie, and I took a walk up the road that runs along the west side of our property, heading toward Superior. Not really looking for anything in particular, I was startled by a giant dragonfly darting right past my head, its tissue paper-like wings barely missing my right ear. My eyes followed its ascent toward the evening sky. That was when I noticed them. The air above the gravel road was filled with big darting dragonflies. I'm guessing when I say there were at least a hundred of them within sight because there was no way to actually count them. They stretched on as far as I could see their dark bodies against the sky as I looked north along the road, and it stayed that way for at least a quarter mile of our walk. Actually, doing the math, there had to have been well over a hundred. Rarely do you see more than a few big dragonflies at any given time, but this I would have to describe as a swarm.

I had seen this same phenomenon once before. I was eating dinner with my family at The Pie Place in the outskirts of Grand Marais, Minnesota, before it moved downtown. We noticed a few dragonflies skimming past the window where we sat. As our gaze moved farther from the building, we realized there were more than we could possibly count. I would say hundreds. We were amazed as we watched the squadron flying past for several minutes, all heading basically northeast, paralleling the north shore of Superior.

In both cases, where they were traveling to or from, I have no idea, but they were definitely on a mission to somewhere. On the side road encounter, I noticed biting insects were pretty much nonexistent during our walk. Whether they were being eaten or just scared into hiding, I didn't know, but I was thankful for the side benefit of our wild encounter.

One snowy November morning during deer season, I was sitting against a tree in the woods behind our house. I don't look for deer when I deer-hunt. Instead I look for anything that catches my attention. As daylight slowly ascended the grayscale, actual features became discernable in the woods. Tree bark became mottled and textured instead of black. The light-gray ground became a rolling white carpet punctuated by rocks and sticks. What caught my attention the most, though, was a slender chocolate-brown form about the size of a house cat that popped in and out of sight as it circled around me, apparently investigating every feature the forest had to offer. With its constant hyperactive movement, even at twenty yards, it was difficult for me to get a clear look. I had my suspicions, but when it finally hesitated for a few seconds while crossing a nearby log, I was able to confirm its identity. It was a pine marten. I had seen them out west before and once at our cabin over in the Tahquamenon area, but this was my first marten sighting nearly in my own backyard. Not long after making my confirmation, it was gone, hunting its way up toward the house. Based on the relatively small size and the fact that I had never encountered it before, even with spending considerable time in the woods, I assumed it was an adolescent that was recently evicted from its birth territory.

My explorations later that morning turned up its tracks over more than ten acres of ground, including our side yard, within twenty feet of our house. Two other sightings in the same area over the course of a few days told me that the elusive little hunter had likely staked a claim on our place and was planning on being a long-term neighbor. I was fine with that. In fact, I was more than fine with it. I was excited about the likelihood of future encounters. Even without regular sightings, our home property feels a little wilder now. That's just one of the benefits of not looking specifically for deer when I am deer hunting. I guess, in a way, it's more like I hunt for wild encounters, which means that I have a lot of successes.

Quite often, when I'm not really looking, the wild UP finds me at home. Whether I'm watching a bald eagle riding invisible thermals high overhead while I'm shoveling snow off our roof or watching a sandhill crane pecking at my window as I sit in my basement office, wild encounters are a welcome distraction from day-to-day responsibilities. I enjoy the relaxation of lying in bed at night with a mild breeze stirring the curtains, listening to the call of an owl somewhere in the night woods and hoping for a response to continue the conversation as I drift off to sleep.

I spend a considerable amount of time exploring fields, forests, and waters from one end of the UP to the other. Through rivers, lakes, bogs, and vast expanses of woods and rugged shorelines, I search out personal experiences with the wild. Quite often, though, it's a two-way trail, as right in or near my own yard, the wild slips in and finds *me*. It may be a freshly bloomed trout lily in the edge of the yard, a feathered miracle gliding overhead, or even evidence of an almost encounter. And I'm not really unique in this area. It happens all over, all the time, here in the Upper Peninsula. They're up close and personal contacts with the wild that catch us by surprise. We may not be able to plan these adventures, but we can certainly enjoy them just the same.

The Greek philosopher Heraclitus is noted to have said, "If you do not expect the unexpected, you will not find it." My paraphrase is "Keep your eyes open for the unexpected." Of course, in this case, spending a lot of time outside ups the odds, but here in the Upper Peninsula, you never know where or when the wild's going to reach out and touch you, whether you're looking for it or not. If you keep an expectant eye out for the unexpected, you're likely not to be disappointed.

Superior Access

*Once you've experienced Superior and the North
Woods, you never really leave them behind.*

It's midafternoon in early May. Snow is gone, for the most part. A
few lingering patches lay scattered through the woods in its deep-
est shadows. Ice formations are still visible on the Big Lake from
M-28 at a number of locations between Munising and Marquette. So
my wife, Julie, and I launch our kayaks into the Laughing Whitefish
River a few hundred yards upstream from the mouth, intent on taking a close-up look at what's going on out in the bay. A slight south-
east breeze still carries a tinge of winter sting. As we peacefully bob
along the edge of a vast collection of floating ice formations, slowly

working their way toward Marquette, I begin thinking of all the different public access points that I know of along the Superior shoreline here in the Upper Peninsula.

A little farther east, Julie and I have floated AuTrain River currents out into AuTrain Bay to paddle along sandy public beaches on a warm summer day. At the far eastern end of AuTrain Bay, in not-so-relaxing weather, we have watched Superior waves crashing against the low cliffs and spraying up into the forest above.

Farther east, we've explored rugged shoreline formations while paddling from the sandy beach at Bay Furnace. Many times, driving along M-28, we have pulled into one of the scenic turnoffs along the lake to watch ominous storm clouds rolling south from Canada, wondering just how wild things were about to become. One time, the storm clouds snuck in on us from the south. We launched our kayaks from the sandy beach near Scott Falls, thinking the gray sky was just going to remain a mellow gray for the afternoon. Checking the weather prediction crossed our minds, but for some reason, we just let the idea come and go. We didn't make it a quarter mile before light sprinkles began changing our outlook. As we looked back toward our put-in point, we saw the dark mass rolling in over the trees. By the time we spun around and started paddling back, slight dimples on the surface of the lake had turned to splashes as drops got bigger and came down faster. By the time we reached shore, there weren't many dry spots left on us for new drops to hit. So we took shelter under the small roof covering the drinking water hand pump to wait for a lull before we put the boats back on our vehicle.

From Sand Point, a few miles out of Munising, all the way over to Grand Marais, Pictured Rocks National Lakeshore holds forty-two miles of Superior trail and boat access. Vehicle access within the Pictured Rocks is limited, but if you're willing to put boots to the trail or a paddle in the water, there's still forty-two miles of Superior shoreline to explore, weather and safety notwithstanding.

AuSable Point lighthouse, part of the Pictured Rocks National Lakeshore, provides prime Lake Superior viewing and access, although it takes a three-quarter-mile hike to reach it, so it's not one of the hop-out-of-the-car locations. To the east is a panoramic view of Grand Sable Dunes sweeping toward Grand Marais. That's where you'll find Log Slide, which is a historic location where logs were slid down the dune to Superior during early logging of the area's old growth forest. Visitors are allowed to make the descent to the lakeside if they choose to, but you had better be in decent shape for the steep climb back up through loose sand. It's one of those one-step-forward, two-steps-back experiences. There is a large sign at the top, warning that the climb out can take up to two hours. I found it to take considerably less than that, but I also do a lot of walking and hill climbing. It's a fun thing to do as long as you are honestly up to it. It's not that the lake really looks any different from that beach than others. It's more the novelty of being able to say that you did it. Most people only do it once.

West of AuSable Point is a combination sand, cobble, boulder, and sandstone shoreline stretching roughly a mile to the Hurricane River mouth. Besides natural attractions, that stretch of beach is also where a few old shipwrecks came to rest. Their ribs still lie partially exposed at water's edge, like wooden skeletons, slowly returning to the earth where their materials originally came from. When we walk that section of beach, I like to linger for a while and imagine the adventures and perils of bygone days.

Near the east edge of Pictured Rocks is a trail that follows Sable Creek out to the lake where Grand Sable Dunes transition back to forested sand. That small stretch of forest leads to the town of Grand Marais, which guards the east side of the park and provides access to multiple beaches, including the beach directly north of town that's known to produce a few agates now and then.

Farther East past a few informal access points is Crisp Point, with its historic lighthouse. Being only a four-and-a-half-mile hike from our cabin through north woods trails, our family has been enjoying visits there for more than twenty years.

Our first view of Crisp Point and its then lonely light tower was from several miles down the beach to the east toward Whitefish Point. When our daughters were young, I would push them in a double stroller equipped with bicycle wheels as we explored trails around the area. We found our way out to an isolated stretch of cobble beach that we always had to ourselves whenever we would visit.

One particularly clear afternoon, we wandered farther west than usual, looking for those ever-elusive agates. Actually, I was looking for agates. Julie and the girls were mostly just looking for whatever interesting things there were to see, which is also a great way to spend a Superior afternoon. Anyway, as I was thinking it was probably about time to turn around and begin the hour-and-a-half trek back to our cabin, I noticed a faint object in the distance that looked like a lighthouse. Julie's always loved lighthouses, but based on the time of day and my estimate of the distance, we decided further investigation would be better saved for another day. Being that we only made it up to our cabin once or twice a year from our home downstate, it took us a couple of years of following trails before "another day" arrived.

I now push my granddaughter on those same trails to Superior in that same stroller that I used to push our kids in. I don't know if the stroller or I will last long enough to bring great-grandchildren to Crisp Point, but I guess things like that aren't for me to worry about anyway. My job is to try to enjoy the moments I have, especially the family moments, and leave the bigger picture up to God.

Once, during a solo visit to our cabin on my way home from helping our daughter Amy move back up to NMU for fall semester, I ventured out to Crisp Point to hunt for agates. After searching near the lighthouse for a couple of hours, I decided to work my way back down to the area where we first noticed the lighthouse from a number of years ago. When you are on your own with no immediate schedule, taking a four—or five-mile stroll down a Superior beach is a natural thing to do. At least for me it is. A few agate-less miles down the beach, I came across a sweeping arc of deer tracks that came out of the woods through a narrow strip of dune grass, skirted the water's edge, then looped back into the woods. From the size and shape of the tracks, I was pretty sure it was a mature buck. Based on the widespread toes, sprayed sand, and distance between tracks, he was running full tilt.

With no trails in the area for major human access, I wondered what could have spooked him so bad that he would be running that hard out here in such a peaceful area. Then I noticed the second set of tracks paralleling his, about ten yards off to one side. In the dry, loose sand of the upper beach, they were nothing more than large roundish pockmarks. Firm, moist sand closer to the water revealed large canine tracks. Living downstate at the time, I first wondered what a big dog could be doing way out here. My brain finally engaged, and I realized I was looking at the long-standing tale of wolf and deer. I never expected to see wolf tracks on a Superior beach. It made the place feel even more wild and remote. I don't know if the event provided a meal for the wolf or an education for the deer, but I know it provided an intriguing encounter for me.

With lighthouse and grounds renovations now in process, Crisp Point is much busier than it was during our earlier visits, but it's still remote enough to be considered off the beaten path—somewhat. As an artist, Julie has used Crisp Point scenes many times to play with on canvas.

Besides Crisp Point, Superior is accessible at numerous lighthouses across the northern Upper Peninsula shoreline. Whitefish Point, which, by UP standards, is not far from Crisp Point, has a nice sand and cobble beach. It's also in a major avian flyway, so it's popular with birders. It can produce the occasional agate as well, for those so inclined. It tends to be busy, though, which is why we don't often visit there, but it does give visitors good exposure to Lake Superior and the entrance to Whitefish Bay. That's where the *Edmund Fitzgerald* was trying to get to in 1975 when it went down in an early November storm. So even though the point may be busy and seem somewhat tame, Superior is not.

A little farther east is Point Iroquois lighthouse. There is a sign there commemorating a fierce Indian battle where Iroquois warriors were massacred by the Ojibway in 1662. It tells stories of early white explorers finding human bones still scattered about the point. The first time we visited, the place gave me a strange feeling, maybe even a bit of uneasiness, like hanging around in an old cemetery at night. It wasn't spooky, just different from the feelings I have visiting Superior at other locations.

Continuing farther east, our family has enjoyed accessing Lake Superior at The Tahquamenon River mouth and Brimley State Park, maybe even a few other places that I've lost track of as well.

Heading west from my daydreaming location near the Laughing Whitefish River's mouth are a few scenic turnoffs along M-28, providing access to Superior. Our youngest daughter and her husband ventured over to one of those locations from Marquette one evening, intending to experiment with taking pictures of the night sky. As a great surprise, they ended up taking pictures of the northern lights. While they were at the beach, the lights didn't look all that impressive due to the sun being in a low-energy cycle. Their camera, though, was able to pick up additional light and color that the naked eye missed. The pictures came out beautiful. It just goes to show you never know just what to expect from an Upper Peninsula Superior encounter no matter how small or insignificant it may seem at first.

Farther west is a long stretch of access from the Visitor's Center in Harvey to the Carp River's mouth. Even though it's all easy access from M-28 / US 41 and the Iron Heritage Trail walking/biking path, when Superior is in a mood, it's still wild and unpredictable. Fish regularly caught there at the Carp River's mouth are plenty wild too. Even along the Marquette waterfront and north along Lakeshore Drive, you can look one direction and see the Marquette cityscape and the NMU Superior Dome, then turn around and wonder at historic structures and the immense untamed wild of Lake Superior. Some days, it appears tranquil and tame, resting lazily around piers and marinas. Other days, it curls its lip and shows the white of its fangs.

One of the Lake Superior lighthouse access points "near" Marquette that stands out in my mind for touching the wild was when I had an opportunity to experience Stannard Rock, dubbed the loneliest lighthouse. I was on a mission to investigate a possible project to monitor fishing for large offshore lake trout. Technically, I guess you can consider Stannard Rock to be a Lake Superior access point, but to reach it, you need a sea-worthy boat to cross some 30 to 50 miles of the lake you want to access, depending on which port you leave from. The rock the lighthouse is built on is actually submerged anywhere from 4 to 16 feet, but I believe there's a small blip showing above the surface, depending on actual water levels at any particular time. Overall, the relatively shallow water of the reef covers an area roughly 0.25 miles by 1 mile. From up on the tower, you can readily see the rocky bottom of Superior around the building foundation of poured concrete.

As our boat neared the isolated structure, it looked like something out of a classic ghost story, complete with a collapsed roof on the entrance room. There was a not-so-inviting aroma due to an abundance of gull guano and the assorted remains of various birds that had made the lighthouse their final stop. The skeleton of what was once a northern flicker rested on the floor of the first tower landing with vibrant yellow wing feather shafts fanned out as if ready to take flight. The view from the tower was what I envisioned it would be like being perched in the crow's nest of a large sailing ship. The dark catacomb basement, which had stagnant puddles covering most of the concrete floor, made the rest of the building seem inviting. I understand that there are plans to refurbish the lighthouse and repurpose it for education and conservation, but I believe those plans are still in their very early stages.

As we boarded the boat and slowly pulled away, it occurred to me that even with this impressive man-made structure standing in defiance, the wilds of Superior still have the upper hand.

Just north of Marquette, Presque Isle is 323 acres of nature, readily available for relaxation and adventure, with numerous places to access Lake Superior. Deer are a common sight. Sightings of moose and bear are not unheard of. Water access runs the gamut from sand beach to cobble to tall cliffs. We've explored them all both on foot and by kayak, but one of my favorite haunts is the break wall. Even though it's a man-made structure, I always enjoy peering into Superior to explore all the nooks and crannies in the submerged boulders. My expectation is to see fish, even though I rarely do. Still, there is something about looking into clear water and letting my mind go down and wander around in the shadows that keeps me coming back.

A little farther north, Sugarloaf Mountain all the way up to Little Presque Isle is a beautiful stretch of Superior shoreline access. Trails run through the area, connecting small hidden beaches and rocky outcroppings. It's picturesque enough that my wife has done paintings of portions of that area.

Even farther north and a little west, Superior is technically publicly accessible along both the Huron Mountains and Huron Islands Wilderness, just not readily accessible. Part of the fun, though, is knowing places like that, truly wild places, exist relatively close to home. The fact that they are there means that they're always a grand Superior adventure possibility.

The Keweenaw Peninsula was my home base for several years during college. Though the area has no shortage of Superior access, most of my visits in those days focused on McClean State Park beach time, fishing for salmon from the breakers at the west end of Portage Canal and climbing the ice formations along the shoreline near Freda and Redridge. Although not necessarily from an academic standpoint, all those areas and adventures contributed heavily to my overall college education.

When I was in graduate school at Michigan Tech, Julie and I would often spend summer Saturdays making "up north" treks into the upper Keweenaw just to leave my studies behind for a while. There were times we would leave Houghton, comfortable in shorts and T-shirts. When we reached the roadside/shoreline park grill where we planned to cook lunch, we had to put on anything else we could find in the truck to wear in order to keep our goose bumps collection to a minimum. Even then, we would end up sitting in our vehicle while things cooked, keeping watch through the windshield and jumping out now and then to flip our meat on the grill. You would think we would have learned after the first incident, but I guess things like that weren't covered in my engineering classes.

On one of those weekend excursions, it was actually warm enough for a swim, or at least the air was. Waves were big enough to be fun to play in without feeling any sense of danger. We worked our way out to about chest-deep water, where we began floating along, bobbing in the waves. Periodically, we would stand up to take a rest. There came a point where we both decided to take a break, only to find we couldn't reach bottom. Surprised, I took a quick look around and realized that, with the waves coming in at an angle, they had pushed us into a small bay where we ended up being much farther from shore than we were originally.

We both got that feeling of panic that comes when you first come to a realization like that. In our slight panic, we got separated in the waves, which suddenly seemed much bigger, adding to the panic. I managed to catch myself before panic completely took over and gave myself a mental slap in the face.

I thought, *I am not going to just quit and let myself drown this close to shore.*

Probably less than a minute later, I did a test reach with one foot and found I could stand up again. When I looked around, Julie was standing not too far away, breathing pretty heavily, having just gone through pretty much the same thing.

The lesson is, you have to pay close attention to the situation and your surroundings when you play in the wild UP because there are risks. During an October storm in 2018, two people drowned at Black Rocks near Marquette when a big wave knocked them down and pulled them in. Pictured Rocks Lakeshore has recently experienced a few serious, or at least near-serious, incidents as well. Superior can be fun and inviting, but it's far from tame.

Speaking of far from tame, Porcupine Mountains Wilderness State Park includes roughly 26 miles of Lake Superior access. Like Pictured Rocks, much of the Porkies shoreline isn't easily accessible, but that's also part of what makes it so appealing. Easy access isn't always the best access.

I personally know of at least 75 public access sites along the Lake Superior shoreline, most of which I've had the privilege of visiting. I'm sure there are many more that I am either not aware of or have forgotten about over the years. I'm not sure how much shoreline frontage that equates to. Once, I started researching locations and doing the math. After coming up with at least 104 miles of publicly accessible shoreline, I decided that the exact number didn't really matter. It's a lot. Lake Superior is accessible—not always easily accessible, but accessible. Again, being readily accessible, though, doesn't mean that it's tame. It's about as tame as a sleeping bear. It can look peaceful and inviting at times, then change moods in short order. The list of lives lost in Superior is long and still growing.

In his book *Breathe the Wind, Drink the Rain*, Douglas Wood exhorts us to "wake up," "attend sunrises," and "unwrap the gift of each day." The Upper Peninsula is a great place to follow his advice, especially along the Big Lake. Having had the privilege to encounter Lake Superior from the Soo Locks to the west end of the Porkies, I've found that, in most places, sunrises and sunsets are typically lightly attended. So front-row seats are still available.

We tend to have our strongest relationships with people like ourselves, probably because we have so much in common. We can easily relate. With our bodies being roughly 65 percent water, why would we not feel a strong relationship with bodies of water? Or should I say *other* bodies of water? It's a natural connection.

It's difficult to have a connection with something you have no access to. Connections foster care and concern for what you're connected to. In his book *Blue Mind*, Wallace J. Nichols conducts an extensive examination of our connection to and with water. In laymen's terms, that special feeling we have around water is *universal*. Who doesn't feel relaxed or at ease around a stream or lake? Superior can be the ultimate in relaxation medicine. Even when it's on edge, pounding shoreline features with white-capped fists, there's something calming in that sense of power. Lake Superior is one of the largest, coldest, and cleanest bodies of fresh water on our planet, and it's readily available. When you connect with cold, clean, fresh water, you're connected with pretty much everything.

Whether you're looking to paddle, do some beach combing, swim, or just visit the water and bask in its immensity, access to one of the great wonders of the UP is readily available and likely not far away. Therapy for what ails your mind is available 24/7. No appointment needed.

On that May afternoon that brought on all this thinking, as we began paddling back toward the river's mouth, ready for dinner, I found myself with another thought. How thankful I was to be living so close!

WILDERNESS WANDERINGS

*In the expanse of the North Woods you can hear your own thoughts.
Past, present and future meet in your mind's eye as you ponder
mysteries of the universe and contemplate the whole of creation or just
simply listen. Amidst the hush, the whisper of God is unmistakable.*

Mention "wilderness," and most people's minds wander off to vast tracts of land out west or in the far north, with a formal federal wilderness designation, places like the Boundary Waters Canoe Area in northern Minnesota, Frank Church River of No Return in Idaho, or maybe the Bob Marshall in Montana, often simply referred to as the Bob. My mind typically treks off to those places too. My body has been blessed to follow at times, providing numerous memorable adventures.

Fortunately, you don't have to travel that far to get your wilderness fix. By my count, there are fourteen wilderness areas right here in Michigan's Upper Peninsula. Most may not be as vast as their federally designated counterparts, but they'll certainly still give you a good dose of wilderness medicine. Here's the list of UP wilderness areas that I'm aware of:

Beaver Basin	11,740 acres
Big Island Lake	5,295 acres
Delirium	11,952 acres
Elliott Donnelley	1,450 acres
Horseshoe Bay	3,842 acres
Huron Islands	147 acres
Isle Royale	132,018 acres
Mackinac	11,363 acres
McCormick	16,925 acres
Porcupine Mountains	42,000 acres
Rock River Canyon	4,722 acres
Seney	25,150 acres
Sturgeon River Gorge	16,744 acres
Sylvania	15,195 acres

If you do the math, that's just shy of 300,000 acres available for exploration and adventure. I haven't personally been to all these wilderness areas yet, but I have had the pleasure of exploring nine of them—some, multiple times.

Rock River Canyon Wilderness is only twenty minutes from my house, so I tend to frequent that area quite often. Fishing the Rock River is my most frequent excuse. Hiking in to hang around at Rock River Canyon Falls is high on my excuse list too. I've hunted deer there a couple of times, but Rock River Canyon venison hasn't yet made it to our dinner table. I'm still working on that.

In many ways, it's not much different than exploring water and woods right out my back door or anywhere else in the UP for that matter. Yet there's something about a tract of land with "wilderness" tagged to its name that sinks its teeth into my imagination, regardless of size.

A couple of years ago, a last-minute change in plans for our daughter and her family meant we wouldn't be babysitting our granddaughter, leaving a big gap in our plans for the day. Finding you have an open day in mid-September, for me, means you have to do something outside—not just outside, but *outdoorsy* outside. I had been wanting to explore McCormick Wilderness for several years. When we moved to the UP, that activity moved to the front page of my to-do list. Somehow, it took nearly two years for it to reach the top of the list, but the day had finally come.

We had to make a couple of stops in Marquette on the way, which, like most interruptions, seemed endless, but we finally embarked on our hike—meaning we crossed the Peshekee River foot bridge—just before noon. Supposedly, the temperature was in the midfifties, but I didn't verify that. I do know that it felt good to slip a fleece pullover on over my flannel shirt, though. It was my drab-green, quarter-zip fleece I've been wearing on backcountry adventures for years. Whenever I put it on, I can feel myself shift into backcountry mode. The same goes for my old green cargo-style pants and L.L.Bean hunting boots, both of which were on my person when we left our truck in the parking lot. Dad's old fixed-blade hunting knife rode on my belt as usual. Wool socks, sage-green Stormy Kromer hat, and red L.L.Bean day pack rounded out my adventure attire. It's not like I can't have an outdoor adventure without this stuff. I just like it.

Being that the main trail to White Deer Lake followed the old McCormick access road to their "camp," it didn't feel as much like wilderness as I expected, but the collection of larger-than-usual trees in the forest—white pine, sugar maple, and yellow birch in the three-foot to five-foot diameter category—identified it as not your typical woods. Places like this are a legacy of those that had money and power to set land aside for recreation and enjoyment instead of plundering it, as was the norm of the times. Even if the "conservation" was for selfish purposes at the time, I appreciate the fact that we all benefit from their wealth and abilities now.

A couple-hundred-yard stretch of what was once trail was submerged in an open marsh, which I assumed was the result of beaver activities at some point. People had made makeshift trails up and over nearby wooded outcrops and hills. I understand that, the following year, National Forest Service staff used mules to haul in supplies to build a boardwalk through this flooded stretch. At the time of our initial visit, though, it was a steep bushwhack.

Near the old McCormick camp, ghosts of old two-tracks dissected the forest. We explored a few, but there wasn't time to satisfy my curiosity on all of them, which means we'll have to go back sometime to pick up where we left off.

We found a yellow birch monarch about five feet in diameter above the root taper, still alive and well. That's getting to be a pretty uncommon tree. Most of the big birches anywhere close to that size range are usually just dead snags waiting to fall. Large white pines seem to show up here and there, but hardwood trees in that category are rare from my experience. So it was an encouraging discovery.

Building foundation ruins dotted the old camp area, along with numerous relics. Wandering among the collection of old foundations in various stages of decay, I tried imagining the camp in its prime— rustic buildings with an elegant air overlooking White Deer Lake and surrounding forest. At one point in my virtual tour, my mind caught a whiff of wood smoke, but returning to crumbling foundations, I found that the only scent that remained was a mingling of woods and water. I was surprised at how much nature had reclaimed what was obviously an extensive building site just since 1987, although that was more than thirty years ago. It just doesn't sound that long ago, at least not to me. Still, it often doesn't take nature long to reclaim things. Even things thought to be long-standing and well established.

I would have liked to see the place before it was dismantled in the late 1980s. We were living in the UP at that time because I was working on a master's degree at Michigan Tech. At the time, though, I didn't even know the McCormick Wilderness existed. The

Keweenaw was the limit of my UP world back then because we didn't have time or money to venture much farther.

Looking down White Deer Lake and eyeing foundation remnants on the rocky island in front of the main camp, I wished we had our canoe with us. The voyager in me wanted to paddle the lake and portage into surrounding waterways. It would be a tough portage to get a canoe all the way into the lake from the parking area, but I'm guessing it would be interesting paddling. I'm also guessing not many people have done it. That alone may be a good reason to give it a try. It's on my list of possibilities.

We plucked a couple of apples from a tree near the old foundations to supplement our lunch. Even though there had obviously been no pruning in a long time, if ever, apples were abundant and of pretty decent quality. For me, apples growing wild and unkept around an old camp or homestead are some of the best-tasting ones. Maybe it's because of the atmosphere of where they're picked, or maybe it's just my imagination. I remember picking some apples from an old tree in an overgrown field while hunting with my dad one time. It was late autumn, and there was light snow on the ground, so the fruit was cold and crisp. Maybe, like good wine, the flavor gets better the longer the memory is stored, but those apples are still my standard of excellence for orchard fruit.

On our return to the trailhead, we took a side trail up to Lower Baraga Lake. It was much less worn than the main trail out to White Deer, which added to its appeal. There were plenty of freshly fallen leaves decorating the forest floor, paving the trail and collecting among boulders in Baraga Creek. They were mostly maples, which are a favorite of mine, but then again, it's tough to rate autumn leaves. They're all appealing in one way or another.

I studied Baraga Creek for signs of fish life—more specifically, trout—as I do all creeks (actually, not just creeks, but moving water in general). Mildly tannin water meandered between dark boulders, collecting browning amber and orange maple leaves. The water felt cool but was not what I would call cold. I guessed it probably wasn't trout water. Then again, that type of thing needs to be investigated. I've found that a four-weight fly rod tends to be a good tool for the job. I did see a ten—or eleven-inch bass in the lake. It wasn't a trout but was still nice to see.

The forest smelled of sweet curing leaves—fern, maple, birch, and a host of others. Maybe that's why I love cooking with basil so much. It has an aroma that reminds me of the autumn woods.

We didn't encounter much in the way of wildlife, except for some birds and chipmunks, although there were signs of beavers, raccoons, and a few others. Somewhere out there are moose too. We've seen them before in the UP but not often, just often enough to keep us looking.

There was another autumn adventure that started on a cool sunny morning full of colorful promise too. It was our first foray into Big Island Lake Wilderness. The two-hundred-yard portage into its namesake lake was scattered with fallen color. We launched into a quiet bay of oval lily pads, burnt red, amber, and green, with multi-pointed stars exploding from their centers. The sky held a scattering of unimposing clouds drifting on a light cooling breeze. Our exploration tour took us from Big Island Lake to Mid Lake, then on to Townline Lake. We circled Townline just for a look-see, then worked our way down the creek connecting to Upper Lake, which is mostly a small wildlife lake where a handful of mallards mingled with water lily flowers that were defying the season. We then backtracked to Mid Lake and on through Coattail Lake into McInnes, where we set up our basecamp for the next couple of days. Our plan was to do a day trip into the southern end of the wilderness the next day for an introductory look around, then work our way back out the following day.

We found a colorful mix of hard and soft maple, birch, aspen, beech, white pine, balsam fir, hemlock, and others—a typical north woods mix for the central Upper Peninsula. The cool breeze was still lingering as we made camp on a ridge some thirty feet or so above the water—the only campsite on the lake. We faced our tent north so we could keep watch for northern lights through the night. Before setting up camp, we enjoyed a late lunch, then settled in for our stay. It was a short trip, so our gear felt unusually light and compact because of the relatively small amount of food and clothes. So far, portages had been short and easy, which came as a nice surprise. We were accustomed to Boundary Waters Canoe Area Wilderness portages, which are often not very short and rarely easy. It was nice to be able to focus on our surroundings during portages and not so much on the hauling or precarious footing.

We took a late-afternoon walk along the ridge above camp, paralleling the lakeshore. There were numerous beaver-felled birch mixed into a stand of small—to medium-sized hemlocks. The birch were probably a hundred yards from the water. We've seen that type of thing before, and I always wonder how the beavers find those trees in the first place. They must roam around away from the water more than I realize, or maybe they can locate their trees of choice by smell. Regardless, it still surprises me when I see it.

Just over the ridge overlooking a swampy creek, we found a forty-inch-diameter white pine stump with a forty-eight-inch-tall balsam fir growing from it. Eventually, it will just be a fir tree growing from a bump in the ground as the original story of the white pine returns to its beginning. I imagine there are countless such stories that I often look right at without recognizing the tale.

I envisioned deer—and other wildlife too—following the boggy creek bottom we were overlooking, so I wandered down for a peek. There was no evidence of a game trail on either side of the creek or bog, but I knew that if I lived out there, I would be stalking its edges.

After dinner, we followed the ridge the opposite direction to find the portage for our next day's journey into the southern lakes. We followed the portage trail for a quick peek at the next lake before returning to camp and collecting some firewood, which was something we should have done earlier. When I get the bug to explore, camp chores sometimes get neglected. During firewood scavenging, we heard a small ruckus. It turned out to be a pine squirrel hauling a white pine cone that pretty much equaled its size. We left the squirrel to its business and headed for camp and our evening fire. Mild weather in an autumn woods, gazing into a crackling fire, is a great recipe for relaxing, dreaming big dreams, and thinking deep thoughts. I always find it tough to let a fire like this die out so I can dowse it and turn in for the night. Just one more log often runs to the end of the pile. I don't want to chance missing a good stream of thoughts.

The next morning was cold and clear. Mist danced and swirled across the surface of the lake. We'd be joining it soon. As our canoe approached the first portage, I saw a moose in the misty water ahead. Then the mist closed in, and I lost sight of it until it emerged again as a stump in sun-glinted water.

We reached Vance Lake by late morning with a half-moon still readily visible, tilting north. A pair of hawks were testing the breeze high above the forest canopy. After a circumnavigational tour, we moved on to Twilight Lake via a roundabout five-eighths of a mile portage.

There, we saw several fish hit something on the water's surface and assumed they were bass. Later, while eating lunch at a campsite, I watched a trout of about eleven inches cruise by and began wondering about my earlier assumption. After watching several more trout cruise past, I changed my assumption and noted Twilight Lake as a trout lake. That note has a star by it in my notebook.

On Byers Lake, I saw two large fish jump in a sizable flotilla of lily pads. Those I assumed were bass. We were surprised to see a house on the southern end of Byers. Out front was a pontoon boat with a 9.5 horsepower motor. I'm guessing it must somehow be grandfathered in because it's fully within what is supposed to be a wilderness area. Regardless of why it was there, it certainly took away much of the lake's appeal. I'm sure the owners like being on that lake, and I guess I can't really blame them for staying there if they can, but we agreed that this would be our only visit to Byers. Houses and motorboats are not what we come to wilderness areas for. We did admit, though, that they had a nice location.

We took the north route out of Byers to get back to Vance. It was a little longer but was new ground to see. Due to high water and lack of trail use, there was a bit of guessing and bushwhacking involved, which is always fun while carrying a sixteen-foot canoe on your shoulders.

Back at Vance Lake, we hooked northeast to investigate the creek and pond up in that area. Wood ducks are apparently fond of it because there were lots of them taking off ahead of us, their mournful cries echoing through the nearby forest. Large mats of floating vegetation with sculpted undercuts and hollows submerged in dark water gave the waterway an almost eerie feel. Quite a ways down the creek, we reached a long beaver dam with a four-foot waterfall on the other side. The creek below looked much too shallow for a canoe, so we took that as our cue to turn around and enjoy the vibrant-color tour back to camp.

As we prepared for our evening campfire after dinner, fish feeding rings pockmarked the silvery middle of McInnes Lake. Dark shoreline reflections framed the scene. I wondered why this rarely happened when I was fishing. Cool darkness began settling in, but the lake didn't look ready to go to sleep. Faint evening stars soon turned to crisp points of twinkling light punctuating the sky. My headlamp spotlighted a gangly-looking snowshoe hare rustling leaves behind our tent as we prepared to turn in for the night. Wilderness sleep came quickly.

Morning dawned cool with a leaden sky—not promising, but not threatening either. Our lake was quiet and still. Looking out over the water from our ridge, I couldn't help but recall Psalm 46:10: "Be still and know that I am God." It set the tone for our relaxed pack-up and reflective journey back to the modern world. Paddling was purposefully slow, and we stopped occasionally to investigate campsites for future possibilities. In the wilderness, I find future possibilities easy to think about and fun to ponder.

As we prepared for our final portage to our vehicle, we were greeted by four guys heading in for a long weekend of fishing. Based on the amount of gear and supplies they were hauling, we surmised they weren't planning to go any farther than one of the two campsites right there on Big Island Lake. They were the only people we had seen other than a couple we had a brief exchange of pleasantries with that had hiked into Vance Lake for a quick look on their way through the area. So for three days, we pretty much had the roughly 5,300-acre wilderness to ourselves. We didn't begrudge the guys spending time on the lake, but we were glad we were heading out as they were heading in.

Of the remaining wilderness areas on the list noted earlier, I've also hiked and kayaked in Beaver Basin, backpacked and canoed on Isle Royale, explored sections of Seney and Sylvania, hiked and fished Elliott Donnelley, and enjoyed considerable time exploring the Porkies on a number of occasions, including being an artist-in-residence to do some writing.

Each area has its own character and its own stories. Thinking back on all of my UP wilderness explorations and adventures, I'm reminded of a comment by conservationist Bob Marshall, who said, "A...singular aspect of the wilderness is that it gratifies every one of the senses." Although that statement may be true for most any natural setting, it's embodied most boldly by true wilderness. The lack of man-made structures and mechanized vehicles puts us on notice that we're someplace different, someplace special. We're freed to let down our social guard and allowed to brush aside certain refinements of civilization. We can lose our shackles of the modern world and step back into our intended role of simply living in the grand scheme of life. We don't have to consciously engage our senses. They come fully alive on their own.

Thoreau is often quoted as saying, "In wilderness is the preservation of the world." I think it's much broader than that. I would say, "In wilderness attributes is the preservation of the world." True wilderness, as I mentioned before, holds special meaning and provides humanity with many benefits, but those benefits don't come exclusively from places carting a wilderness moniker. Those intangible benefits were built into all of creation. In developed areas, wildness of nature has just become so fragmented and diluted that it's difficult to recognize. Even in the busiest cities, it still exists in the form of streetside trees, flowers, and small parks. It oftentimes doesn't take a large area of wildness to penetrate our civilized modern selves and touch the part of us that still clings to our roots, our beginning, as part of the natural world. We were created to be an integral part of and work with and within nature. Some of us have strayed farther from our roots than others, but I don't believe any of us are completely out of touch with where we started as human beings.

The beauty of the UP is that there are opportunities at all levels to connect or reconnect with our natural world. Whether your idea of wilderness is an untamed area where you can spend a day, or days, on your own, or a small-scale natural rendezvous within sight of your vehicle, the wild is always waiting to welcome us home.

EVEN AROUND TOWN

Up North, things are different. Which things and what exactly is different isn't always clear, but something's different. It just feels like Up North, even in town. In some ways, it may look and smell of Up North too. Regardless, there's no mistaking it. You're Up North and that's good. Maybe you're on vacation. Maybe you're home. Maybe both. But, you're Up North and you're glad to be here.

The doe eyed us suspiciously as we stood watching from the trail about twenty yards away. She didn't seem to be very nervous, but I could tell she didn't exactly trust us either. It was our third close deer encounter within about fifteen minutes. We weren't on a back-country hike or even looking for deer for that matter. We were just enjoying a fringe benefit of sneaking in a short walk on the well-used trails of Presque Isle Park in the outskirts of Marquette. Without walking all that far, we could have also been admiring intricate lichen patterns on weathered rock formations or watching thundering waves do their work on shoreline cliffs.

We don't always have time to venture off into the outback wilds, but that's one of the things I love about the Upper Peninsula. It feels like you're up north and within reach of the wild even when you're around town. After all, most UP towns are basically just openings in the forest where a relative handful of buildings reside. Even in towns large enough to be referred to as "cities," you're typically never more than ten minutes from being out of town. Deer, bear, and bald eagle sightings around towns are relatively common, and moose sightings are not unheard of in some areas.

With many small UP towns, and some not-so-small towns for that matter, nestled into the surrounding wilds, it's sometimes difficult to tell exactly where the wilds end and town begins. In some ways, they're part of each other, which is maybe how it should be. The same goes for personal property, whether it's around town or not. We let our yard gradually emerge from the surrounding forest instead of having straight, well-defined delineations. Some parts of our yard look like the forest, and some parts of the forest are actually yard as far as I'm concerned. At some point back in time, all this land was wild and untamed, simply belonging to the world at large. So in a way, we're all basically just squatters living on land we don't truly own. Whether town governments or private citizens, we're just temporary caretakers of various parcels of land, working diligently to keep nature at bay. If you don't think so, try a little experiment. Stop mowing for a while. Quit pruning, picking up branches, and spraying chemicals around, and see how long it takes the wild to creep back in and take over. Based on my experience, not long.

The wilds are typically closer than we sometimes realize. Once, when my wife, Julie, was working on a plein air painting in front of the Marquette lighthouse, I was roaming the grounds, trying to stay out of her way. I ended up spending part of my time sitting on a ragged waterside rock and watching a loon cruising the shoreline, seemingly unconcerned about my presence. It caught me by surprise because I've always considered loons to be part of wilderness settings or, at the very least, quiet, secluded lakes, not a city waterfront. Unlike gulls, who seem to divide their time between cruising the shoreline and squabbling over discarded french fries in the local McDonald's parking lot, loons usually tend to shy away from around-town activities. Regardless of why it was there, I just considered the encounter to be one of those unexpected and undeserved blessings we sometimes get to enjoy.

One summer day up on Sugarloaf, a rocky overlook not much farther out of Marquette than Presque Isle, a flash of iridescent blue caught my attention. What I saw were the stripes on a striped skink. At the time, I had no idea striped skinks even existed in Michigan, let alone the Upper Peninsula. They look like something you'd expect to see in the arid southwest states or maybe even somewhere exotic. Turns out they're just an exotic-looking UP native.

I was treated to a short stare-down with a saw-whet owl in a spruce thicket in the Chocolay Bayou Community Forest, which is surrounded by the community of Harvey, within sight of Marquette. In the same general area, along the Iron Heritage Trail paralleling US 41, I've enjoyed picking and munching on fresh Thimbleberries while helping a Superior Watershed Partnership crew pull invasive weeds and plant native wildflowers. That's right near the whitewater mouth of the Carp River, where people fish for wild steelhead and salmon.

In the western outskirts of Marquette, I've stood overlooking a small brook trout stream, talking about habitat improvement efforts with a DNR fisheries biologist. If it wasn't for a relatively narrow swath of trees, we would have been watching traffic go by on US 41 while we talked. Not far north, the Upper Peninsula Land Conservancy is working on developing a Dead River Community Forest. The Dead is a river that outdoors writer Jerry Dennis once noted must have been named by a fisherman to keep other people away. It's like a lot of UP streams—close at hand, well known by name, but is more of a general acquaintance to most people as opposed to a close friend.

Besides Marquette, Munising is another good example of the even-around-town scenario. For starters, at least half a dozen waterfalls are scattered around the outskirts. One, Alger Falls, is readily visible as you drive by on M-28, just east of town. At church one Sunday,

Pastor Kelto commented that he couldn't believe how many tourists stop and get out of their vehicles to get a better look and take pictures of the falls that are right in the edge of town. Sometimes during the peak summer season, it actually causes a minor traffic issue. His point turned out to be how sometimes we overlook the blessings we have right in front of us. To most locals, the Alger Falls is just a fact, like a curve in the road or a billboard. To visitors, though, having a cascading waterfall alongside of the main road right in the edge of town is pretty spectacular, even worth stopping and getting out of the car for. Having only lived here for a few years now, I'm somewhere between a local and a visitor. I certainly consider myself a local, but I'm still easily impressed with the natural attractions. My hope is to never lose that sense of wonder and excitement for the area.

Munising Falls is another of the near-town natural attractions. We visit fairly often because Julie likes to take pictures of the falls in various conditions to use as references for some of her paintings. She's always looking for variations in light interacting with the falling water, sandstone cliffs, and nearby vegetation. I usually focus my attention on Munising Creek, below the falls, in its serpentine descent toward Superior. Even though I rarely see anything in the way of aquatic life in its small riffles, runs, and holes, I always have to look.

One September afternoon, we stopped by for a quick photo visit. I habitually scanned the creek as we made our way up the path to the falls, my brain cruising on autopilot. An out-of-place grayish patch snapped me back to cognoscente mode in time to recognize the form of a fish gently swaying its tail near a miniature logjam. I was surprised to find myself looking at a coho salmon. In fact, I soon found that I had discovered a pair of coho in a hop-across width creek in the edge of town. Several people walked past, apparently oblivious to nature's drama unfolding in the creek, as I stood there wondering why I hadn't brought my fly rod.

Besides waterfalls, Munising has Grand Island, which is part of the Hiawatha National Forest, perched right in its window to the north. We've explored the island's eastern shoreline by kayak, launching our boats near the ferry dock just west of town. On the island, we've hiked a good portion of the more than forty miles of trails without much company—well, except for a bear. In winter, the island is home to an interesting collection of ice caves created by water seeping from the sandstone cliffs. When Munising Bay freezes solid enough for safe crossing, the ice formations can cause quite a collection of spectators as well.

In a more consistently accessible area, I've enjoyed technical ice climbing just outside of town on cliffs along Sandpoint Road, right across Munising Bay from Grand Island. The ice formations are only a hundred yards or so from the road. Hardly wilderness, but you wouldn't know it from the ice formations or the cliffs they're clinging to. Near the end of climbing one evening, we could feel the chill that accompanies the warm glow of sunset, even tucked into the edge of the forest like we were. From the top of the climb, we could see it—a mingling of amber, orange, and red highlighting the western sky above Superior. Sunset has a way of seeping in and taking hold of your imagination whether you're basking in wilderness solitude or perched near the edge of town. At least it does with me.

Atop of those same cliffs runs a portion of Munising Ski Trails. One autumn day, we hiked the ski trails for a different perspective. I tried for a while to identify some of the winter climbing routes from the top, but it's completely different without snow and ice. My mind kept skipping ahead to winter, envisioning challenges of climbing and skiing. Fall is my absolute favorite season, and it tends to be as fleeting as a bag of M&M's with a bunch of kids around, so I abandoned searching for ice climbs and got back to living autumn moments, leaving winter thoughts for the coming winter.

On the opposite side of the solar cycle, I think of springtime in Houghton. More specifically, I think of a small stair-stepping creek running through the residential section of town, working its way toward the Portage Canal. I walked past it every day on my way to and from campus when I was a student at MTU. It was like a small water garden right adjacent to the road. Which road it was, I don't recall. Road names, especially in town, don't usually stick with me. It doesn't matter. What mattered were the small plunge pool I could peer into but couldn't quite make out the benthic features of and the rocky creek bed and pussy willows lining each bank. As I walked down a paved street, burdened with thoughts of studies and test schedules, that oasis always allowed me to escape to the freedom of wilderness thoughts for a moment. It was on private property, but trespassing with your eyes isn't a crime (as long as you're not looking through somebody's window).

Just east of Houghton is another flowage, the Pilgrim River, which passes through the Nara Preserve as it empties into Portage Canal, creating an open door for one of the few remaining coaster brook trout populations along Superior's south shore. Regrettably, when I was a student at MTU, that close-at-hand connection to the wild went unnoticed by me. My primary outdoors focus tended to be north, up the length of the Keweenaw Peninsula. In more recent years, though, the university and the Copper Country Chapter of Trout Unlimited are changing that with coaster research and a large community forest along the river corridor. I periodically conduct my own studies there now with fly rod and reel. I'm not exactly making up for lost time, but then again, you never really do.

A little farther north, I was poking around on the Eagle Harbor public beach one sticky August morning while Julie was preparing her booth for the town's annual art fair. The beach was anything but wild or rugged; it was complete with park benches and swimming markers. As I paced along the waterline, grasping for a connection to something bigger, something beyond sitting in a crowded park while trying not to sweat, I found it, or more appropriately, it was given to me in the form of a small red-orange agate chip. Half the size of my pinky fingernail, it stood out boldly among the coarse grains of sand. Superior was breathing gently, its waterline barely ebbing back and forth half an inch. I was so surprised to find it there that I just stared at it for a few seconds, blinking as if it might just be a mirage. It wasn't. It was a gift—a red-orange spark to spur adventurous thoughts to get me through the day.

Here in the Upper Peninsula, I've found sparks like that are not uncommon. They're all around, waiting for us to make the connection. They're little glimpses of the wild, brief brushes with adventure, small gateways to big thoughts, vast wilderness, and seemingly endless waterways. Even around town.

GHOSTS OF FORESTS PAST

Once upon a time, they were monarchs of the wild. Branches stretching out like wings of the eagles soaring past. Legions upon legions covering the landscape. Now, jagged stumps, fire-scared and hollow, with grey fingers grasping at the sky. Scattered across the landscape through forest and field, they're hosts to insects, lichens, and moss. A new generation of saplings growing from within, quietly reach back to the sun. They're the ghosts of forests past. Reminders of what once was.

When we bought our property near Tahquamenon Falls twenty-some years ago, we were primarily attracted to the woods, and large meadows filled with ferns and wild blueberries. We were drawn to the peaceful isolation. Though not necessarily a draw, one of the features that intrigued me was the stumps. I'm not talking about resprouting maple stumps from recent logging. I'm talking about big charred pine stumps that dotted the meadows, nearing the end of their long journey back to the earth. Those stumps held stories—stories of two-man crosscut saws, plaid wool shirts, stout horses, and tall-wheeled carts; stories of tall canopies soaking in sunlight and the sacred hush of a forest floor thick with the duff of fallen pine needles. Sometimes I would stand at the edge of one of our meadows, usually late in the evening, gazing out at the collection of grayed and blackened stumps peeking out of their cover of ferns and berry bushes, and wonder what it was like once upon a time, when giants with outstretched arms touching finger-to-finger stretched out of sight in every direction.

There are still places in the UP that offer glimpses of that once-upon-a-time landscape. Estivant Pines is one of those places. It's two hundred acres of what was once the entire Keweenaw. One particular tree was measured at nearly eight feet in diameter above the root spread. A chunk of that tree lying on its side in an average home would nearly brush the ceiling. Standing in the shadows of the collection of giant white pines in the Estivant sanctuary, I've tried to envision a forest of such monarchs spreading down the Keweenaw, across the UP, and down through the Lower Peninsula. It's intriguing to think about, but I can't quite wrap my mind around it because it's too far removed from the reality of today. Truly big trees are relatively small in number now, so they don't really do justice to conveying the magnitude of what once was.

The reason any of these trees still exist at all in the Estivant tract is likely due to multiple changes of ownership and the fact that, during the logging and mining booms of the 1800s, local focus was tilted more toward copper than pine. Still, we are fortunate this remnant escaped the saw, regardless of why. While the surrounding forest is dotted with stumps, both old and new, Estivant Pines is a place we can go to see what once was and dream about what could be, although I'm not sure, in our current environment, if trees of those proportions are even possible today.

Farther east, we spent a few days in Big Island Lake Wilderness one September. Camped at a site on a ridge overlooking Mcinnes

Lake, one evening, we took a walk to explore the ridge and marshy valley below. The surrounding forest was a mix of autumn colors, accented with evergreens of various shades. Perched in the edge of a small opening, just off the spine of the ridge, we came across a roughly four-foot-diameter stump halfway through its return to the soil. Based on what remained of the wood, I believe it was a white pine. I doubt it was one of the virgin timber giants but certainly a respectable tree in its day. I could see it poised there high on the ridge, overlooking the valley concealing a boggy creek. Probably others of its kind were sharing the sunny ridge as they reached for the sky.

A four-foot-tall balsam fir grew from the punky center of the stump that was more soil than wood. The small sapling stood straight as it took its turn in the long forest succession of reaching toward the sun. An array of green and yellow-green lichens shared the gray host stump, working in harmony with the elements to finish the stump's journey back to the earth it came from—not quite full circle yet but closing the gap. Someday, the scene will be of a medium-sized fir tree growing from a mound of rich soil. Eventually, the mound will all but disappear, taking with it the old white pine that once stood tall along the ridge.

Tyoga Historical Pathway is another place where forests past and present intermingle. Originally part of the Tyoga Lumber Company's 7,000-acre tract in the early 1900s, this 200-acre piece of Escanaba State Forest in Onota Township is now home to a 1.6-mile trail loop that includes interpretive signs commemorating various aspects of the historic mill and lumbering town. The once-busy community only lasted for about two years. Part of the stone steam-engine foundation that sits near the bank of the Laughing Whitefish River is the only physical remains of Tyoga's dashed dreams. On the north end of that trail just east of the river is a stand of large hemlocks where one can still catch just a hint of that primeval feel of the prelogging forest. The shadowed forest floor is soft with an accumulation of over a hundred years of decaying hemlock needles and branches. Trunks of large trees no longer able to withstand the elements lay in various stages of decay. Moss-covered boulders lay scattered through the landscape, and a small creek gurgles between roots, then cascades down toward the river.

In a 2017 October storm, one of the big hemlocks fell across the trail. A section of trunk was cut to reopen the trail, providing an opportunity for a history lesson. Near as I could tell, it had 110 rings about 30 feet above ground level. Assuming it took roughly 30 years for the tree to reach that height would put the tree at about 140 years old. I estimated the trunk near the base to be about 32 inches in diameter. Tyoga logging ceased in 1907, which was 110 years before the tree blew down. That would mean that the tree may have been 20–30 feet tall during Tyoga logging and somehow escaped being crushed as giants around it were felled.

Old photographs show no trees at all near the buildings, so this tree must have been just outside the formal settlement. Early accounts talk of Tyoga loggers cutting trees 5 and 6 feet in diameter. Forests of trees of that magnitude are difficult to imagine, but standing there in the Tyoga hemlock cathedral, I can squint my eyes and see them stretching out in great multitudes.

Periodically, I do some trail cleanup around the pathway. It feels strange to fire up my chainsaw with its harsh modern scream. It somehow seems wrong to drown out the natural sounds. In fact, I feel a little embarrassed about doing it, but as soon as I shut off the engine, the ancient voices return, whispering through needle-covered branches, sharing tales rarely heard in modern times.

In some ways, I blame early loggers for our loss of virgin forests, but then I realize they were just trying to survive, like many of us. Then I boil over the greed of early logging companies. But then again, conquering the wilderness was the cry of the time, driven by the credo of Manifest Destiny, and building the economy was a top priority. Trees of the vast forests seemed inexhaustible, like bison, passenger pigeons, and grayling. I'd like to think we've learned our lesson, but sometimes I'm not so sure. Some of us have. Many have not. Exploiting our natural resources isn't just a thing of the past. Maybe one of the reasons for our lack of understanding past mistakes is that many of the scars have healed up so nicely. Thick green summer forests and beautifully colored autumn attire hides our once-wounded landscape. In many places, the old scars are still there; they're just not readily visible unless you roam the woods and fields, searching them out.

An area where you don't have to search very hard is the Kingston Plains, located toward the east end of Pictured Rocks National Lakeshore. After all the virgin timber was logged, scorching wildfires and erosion ravaged the area, essentially sending the land back to ground zero as far as rebuilding the soil to the point where it could once again support much of any plant or tree life. It's now prime berry-picking real estate, and in some ways, the semi-open plains, dotted with gray weathered stumps and supporting a varied mosaic of relatively young regrowth, has an aesthetic appeal. When you compare it to an area of normal regrowth after more recent logging, though, you begin to get a feel for how slow the recovery has been and just how devastated the area must have been after removal of virgin timber, with subsequent fires and erosion. But in a much bigger timeframe than we as individual humans are used to, it's beginning to progress through the stages of regeneration, on its way back to a mature pine forest. It certainly will not complete the journey in any of our lifetimes, but it's on its way.

Ultimately, we need to forgive the unbridled sins of the past grievous trespasses against creation and, as Aldo Leopold advocated, work to build a relationship with the land. That relationship needs to include the lives of all who depend on the land for survival. Plant life, animal life, and human life need to once again blend together as integral parts of the whole. In this now broken and imperfect world, we'll likely never be able to restore the original harmony that once existed, but I believe that's the goal we need to set our sights on, lest the ghosts of forests past become the only forests future generations know.

For now, as mentioned earlier, there are still big trees to be seen in the Upper Peninsula. Maybe they're not of the old growth forest caliber but are still majestic in their own right. The Sylvania Wilderness comes to mind, as does Porcupine Mountains Wilderness State Park. Beaver Basin Wilderness, which is within the Pictured Rocks National Lakeshore, has its share of big trees too. It not only has white pine and hemlock but also has sugar maple and yellow birch as well. Rock River Canyon Wilderness and McCormick Wilderness both hold a good collection of large trees, but they are not as readily accessible as some other areas. In some ways, though, lack of accessibility makes them more attractive to me. It's not that the other trees are lacking because of their location, but like many things, having to work harder to get to them makes for a more rewarding experience.

AuTrain Island is said to hold some big trees. In fact, I've heard people use the term "old growth," but being a private island and a little too far offshore to be readily and safely accessible by me in my paddle-powered watercraft, I'll just have to take the comments at face value and let it go at that. The island does always catch my eye, though, and my imagination for that matter, every time I pass it when traveling M-28. Maybe someday I'll get a chance to take a look.

There is also still old-growth timber, in the form of logs, submerged in Superior and likely buried in some of our rivers as well. They are lost links to past forests, treasures hidden away in cold storage. We have a cutting board made from old-growth wood salvaged from Superior by a company that used to be in Ashland, Wisconsin. I don't believe the company is still in existence, but the cutting board is still on display in our dining area. The wood is beautiful!

As I explore the Upper Peninsula, I'm noticing large old deteriorating tree stumps everywhere—Rock River Canyon, Kingston Plains, Big Island Lake, Keweenaw, Forest Reserve property, Tahquamenon Falls, Tyoga, Hiawatha National Forest—which makes sense since pretty much the entire UP has been logged at least once, several times in some places. Even areas with beautiful forests are not what they once were. The face of the land has been altered. Forests of the past are but ghosts rattling around in old photographs and artwork.

Many forests across the Upper Peninsula, as elsewhere, have regenerated into beautiful woodlands, as they were designed to do. New recruits have taken the places of fallen monarchs. Having never seen the UP in its old-growth pine attire, we have nothing to compare its current state with. Even "large" forests of today only cover hundreds or even a few thousand acres of unbroken landscape. It's difficult to fathom hundreds of thousands of acres or more of unbroken forest. In my mind, the tranquility of a mature stand of hemlocks, with its softness of light and sound, occasional shafts of sunlight penetrating the cool air, is how I envision the look and feel of virgin pine forests—hushed, with a sense of timelessness. Other than through written accounts, though, we'll never know the forests that once were. We can only enjoy what we have, work to be good stewards of these gifts, and be thankful we at least have some treasured reminders of what once was.

So whenever I get an opportunity to visit one of the old-growth remnants, I try to engage all my senses, then let my mind journey back to the once-upon-a-time world of the ghosts of forests past.

Chasing Hoofprints

*Sometimes, death is nature's way of creating
opportunities for new beginnings.*

Having been involved with deer hunting for nearly fifty years,
when we first looked at the UP property where we now live, I
couldn't help but notice the muddied deer trails running down the
middle of all the old logging trails around the property. Dreams and
schemes started swirling in my head. Neither one of us had actually
verbalized it, but I think my wife, Julie, and I were both leaning
toward making an offer on the place as we walked the trails one more
time. Casually glancing off through a patch of aspen, I spotted several
pointed white "branches" sticking an inch or so out of the ground-
cover. Without consciously thinking about it, my brain immediately
connected the dots and recognized what I was looking at.

"That's a nice buck!" I exclaimed as I quickly walked in that direction.

Thinking I was talking about a deer on the hoof, Julie thought maybe this house hunting had finally gotten to me and that I was heading off into the woods to try to run him down. Before she got too concerned, I reached down and lifted my prize up for her to see. It was a heavy ten-point rack still attached to the skull it once grew from or at least what was left of the skull. The antlers were weather-bleached but still solid.

"Does this mean we're buying the place?" Julie asked.

I thought of that buck and some of the gnarly old UP bucks I'd seen in vintage photos as we wrote an offer the next day.

The reality of selling our farm downstate, cleaning out twenty years' worth of accumulation, packing, and actually moving took another six months—until Thanksgiving weekend, to be exact. I made sure I knew exactly where my hunting stuff ended up in the unloading process. Julie didn't seem at all surprised when I began negotiating time off from unpacking and rearranging our belongings to slip in a little hunting during the last three days of the regular firearm deer season. After more than thirty years of marriage, I think she's got me pretty well figured out, at least from that respect.

The first time I ventured out on our new property felt like opening day when I was fourteen years old, stumbling wide-eyed into my first real deer season as an actual hunter instead of an excited spectator. Also, much like my first venture into deer hunting, those first three hunting days produced a distant fading-light glimpse of two does as my only success. Muzzle-loader season produced another two doe sighting and I was pretty sure it was those same two. Compared to my Jackson County farm field days of watching a collection of twenty-five to thirty deer jockeying around in front of me, the experience was a little deflating to say the least. I hadn't done any big-woods whitetail hunting in well over twenty years. It was long enough that I was back near the front end of the learning curve, but I figured I had enough experience now to accelerate the learning pace considerably. I had about nine months to think things through and piece together a plan before archery season rolled around.

That first winter was fairly mild in terms of both temperature and snowfall, so we continued to see fresh deer tracks in our trails on a regular basis. Frequent deposits of fresh tracks continued through summer and early autumn, accompanied by periodic backyard sightings, especially once our few apple trees started dropping samples on the ground. As my first full UP deer season approached, I hung four tree stands, strategically located along our well-used trails. I even bumped into a few deer while hauling stands around, including a couple of small bucks right near our yard, as I was returning from hanging stands. One was a three-point, and the other looked like a small six-point. I spied on them for fifteen or twenty minutes before leaving them to their business and heading to the house for lunch, thinking that hunting prospects were looking promising.

Early during archery season, I saw a lone small doe trot past me in one of my tree stands like she'd been spooked. I waited in anticipation for the source of the spooking, but it never materialized. The rest of bow season slipped by without another sighting except for periodic backyard visitors, which my wife usually told me about when I came in from hunting.

The report was usually something like "There were three does in the backyard about twenty minutes ago."

I saw the tracks. I saw the rubs. I saw the scrapes. The only deer I saw, though, were in my mind's eye and our backyard floodlight.

Gun season, ditto, except for the addition of a brief flash of a white flag through a thick screen of spruce. Muzzle-loader season came and went without even the brief flash of white. Patiently sitting and waiting in strategic locations, which had worked so well for me down in farm country, wasn't panning out so well up here in the big north woods. I knew from the beginning that not using bait like most everyone else put me at a disadvantage. I just hadn't comprehended the magnitude of that disadvantage. Another season, a full season this time, nearly two and a half months, had been spent being in the right place at the wrong time. Then again, if deer weren't showing up during shooting light, maybe I wasn't in the right place. Regardless, telltale tracks with no sightings provided the revelation that something needed to change. Location, timing, technique—something needed tweaking. Or maybe I needed a complete overhaul. I had another nine months to work through the frustration and hopefully figure things out.

Another mild winter of fresh tracks led to another spring and summer of well-worn deer trails down the middle of all our wide access trails left over from previous logging. When it came time to hang tree stands again around Labor Day, I decided to cut back to only two instead of my usual four. I actually thought about skipping the stands altogether, but I just couldn't bring myself to do it. Thirty-plus years of hunting from a tree stand during bow season is a hard habit to break. So I picked two prime locations, one along a well-used trail and one along the edge of a small aspen clear-cut we had done the previous winter. Facing the other direction from the clear-cut was a shaded hardwood ravine with a small creek meandering through the bottom, crossed by a well-used game trail. Both stands looked and felt like good places to see deer.

When I sat in the stands for a few minutes just after hanging them, I envisioned where I would most likely see deer in the coming weeks—and not just deer; bucks. A tinge of confidence crept in. No shooting shack. No bait. Just me and the woods and the deer… Something told me this was the year for fresh venison steaks. Maybe it was just wishful thinking. Maybe the lack of seeing deer was messing with my mind, like how you start to see things in total darkness just because your brain can't handle having nothing to see. Either way, I enthusiastically charged into the season.

One mid-October morning, after the leaves had started thinning out, I finally saw a buck from one of my stands. Two bucks, in fact. They were small, one was a three-point, and the other was a fork-horn, but they were bucks nonetheless. Of course, with the combo tag I had purchased, they weren't legal bucks, but at least things were moving in the right direction. They browsed past at fifty or sixty yards, giving me a twenty-minute show. A third deer, larger no doubt, was making noises in a thicker stand of trees not far from the other two, but he never joined the show. Still, I was getting closer to a successful UP deer season.

Later that morning, I slipped down out of my stand and snuck back to the house, full of hope and anticipation. I was confident that my transition to becoming a UP deer hunter was nearly complete.

For the remainder of bow season, twice I encountered glowing eyes in our backyard on my way out for a morning hunt. Another morning, while sneaking through the predawn woods, I had a button buck come from at least sixty yards away. It looked right at me the entire time, apparently mesmerized by my headlamp beam, and passed by me less than five yards away. I had no shot opportunities, but at least I was having actual deer encounters to keep me motivated.

Early in gun season, I was leaning against an aspen one morning, fending off shivers, waiting for the relative warmth of daylight. Only by spending considerable time in the woods over a lengthy span of hunting seasons, typically with rain, snow, or sleet tickling my nose, have I come to understand the true time involved in that morning transition from dark to light. It's like watchfully waiting for water to turn to ice when you're in need of an ice cube. Here in the north woods, it isn't difficult to tell when the process is complete, though. You can usually feel it in your toes.

About the time colors finally became distinguishable, brown furry movement caught my attention. It was darker in color and smaller than I was hoping for, but it took my mind off the cold. A few brief glimpses gave me enough clues to be able to identify my visitor as a pine marten. After it hunted its way out of sight, I began my slow, methodical, quiet stalk through our woods. I studied new tracks in the snow, visited old rubs, and slowly patrolled the trails, which were really the only places I could get a shot more than about fifteen yards if an opportunity arose, which it didn't.

The next day was a repeat, including the marten encounter. My bow season enthusiasm was beginning to wane, and I found myself wondering if this was just going to be another season spent chasing hoofprints.

The next time I was able to get out and hunt, it was cold, windy, and snowing off and on all day. I spent over twelve hours still-hunting our woods with nothing to show for it except for being damp and chilled, but I did actually see (and even had a shot at) what I believed was a legal buck at about eight thirty in the morning. After sitting near the junction of two major trails for the first couple of hours, I snuck down into our Christmas tree meadow for a look around because that seemed to be somewhat of a crossroad for deer activity. As I stood by a couple of big spruce trees in the middle of the small meadow, thinking about what I wanted to do (and feeling a little disgusted with my lack of success), there was a commotion of crunching icy snow and breaking branches behind me.

I turned around to see a doe pop out of the thick woods and trot away up the trail I just came down. Twenty yards behind her was a small buck. He stopped broadside on the trail and looked at me for a few seconds. I was tempted to go ahead and pull the trigger, but I just couldn't see his antlers good enough to count points. Having a combo tag, he had to have at least three points on one side. I thought he did, based on the short naked-eye side view I had as he trotted from the trees and deadfall, but I just could not tell for sure. As I contemplated shooting, my mind jumped back and forth between yes and no until he made my decision for me and trotted up the trail in pursuit of the doe. I hurried in that direction just in case. As I closed the gap, the doe, who had looped to the west, popped back across the trail about fifty yards in front of me with the buck still in hot pursuit twenty yards behind her. I tried to stop him three times by making doe bleat sounds, but he never paid any attention as he dashed back into the thick woods they had emerged from a minute or so earlier.

The last time I saw them, they were a hundred yards away, snaking uphill through the woods, heading for somewhere other than where I was. I just stood there, somewhat stunned, not knowing what to say, thinking about how I probably just blew the first legitimate shot I had in nearly two years. A few words did come to mind, but I won't mention them. Not knowing whether to kick myself for missing an opportunity or congratulate myself for not panicking and possibly shooting an illegal buck, I just continued on still-hunting our trails, reliving the encounter in my head again and again, still trying to count antler points.

Late afternoon found me haunting our east border and exploring out into the timber company lands adjacent to us. The day ended with me back in the edge of our Christmas tree meadow, crusted with ice and snow as I watched darkness creeping in, alone and shivering, with success still out there running around in the woods.

A couple of days later, I was back in the woods. Again, it was cold, windy, and snowing—typical UP winter weather. By early daylight, I was fighting off shivers again, and my fingers were beginning to hurt, so I started my still-hunting routine a little earlier than usual. First, I snuck down into our Christmas tree meadow, where I pondered my choices for a few minutes, then slowly crept north on a trail following the edge of our cedar/hemlock swamp. I didn't get far before a doe darted across about a hundred yards in front of me. She came out of the deadfall jungle east of the trail and dropped down into the cedar swamp on the west. She looked like she was being pursued, so I got my rifle ready and waited. After a minute or so of nothing happening, I cautiously moved forward another thirty or forty yards.

That was when the buck came trotting up the trail toward me and then peeled off toward the west and stopped, gazing intently into the swampy woods where the doe had disappeared. He had a stout body but not much for antlers. I saw three points on the small main beam as he made his turn just before stopping, so I centered my scope on the middle of his chest and squeezed the trigger on the little .308. Even though it was my doing, the abrupt bark of the gun caught me a little by surprise. The buck jumped and kicked out with his hind legs, then disappeared into the thick woods. The sound of a crash in dead branches came seconds later, followed by what sounded like a hush compared to the recent noise.

Instinctively, I racked the bolt, pocketed the spent silver casing, and slowly moved forward. On my way to the point of impact, my mind started messing with me, and I debated in my head whether I had actually seen three points or not. I knew I did. At least I was pretty sure I knew I did. Standing there by the few tufts of hair and red-speckled snow, looking into the tangled swamp, I was excitedly hopeful but still had a tinge of doubt.

The trail was easy to follow. A blood-sprayed cedar told me he wasn't far. I readily found the matted patch of snow where he went down. The area was smeared with black mucky streaks, but there was no deer. Then I spotted his brown form in the snow just a few yards farther, on the other side of a small spruce. Through the blur of branches, ears were readily visible, but no antlers. A slight feeling of panic set in. I peeked around the spruce to get a clearer view. A short curved reddish antler with three short points brought a sigh of relief. I don't think I've ever been so elated to see a small buck. As it turned out, he sported inch-long brow tines as well. He had started the season as a small eight-point, but apparently, a fight reduced the formal count to seven. I had no issues with that! He was a legal buck; a beautiful little legal buck; the first from our U P property.

I admired him for a few seconds before I took a knee to say my thank-you prayer as a north wind whispered his eulogy through the towering hemlocks. His blue-gray eyes were like holes into outer space. They gave me the feeling of looking into infinity. I wondered if I had seen that particular blue gaze shining at me in the backyard floodlight one of those numerous times I turned it on to monitor nighttime activity around our apple trees. Then I recalled the blue shining stare of that little button buck that strolled by me in the woods that morning during archery season.

Tufts of snow fell from surrounding evergreens as I pulled out Dad's old 1960s vintage hunting knife. The dark curved blade Dad had blued with gun-bluing back in the '70s showed a few worn streaks of bare steel, but it did its job once again. I'll never know the knife's full history, but that's part of the appeal. Hopefully, my kids will have the same sentiment when, someday, it gets passed on to them.

After wrestling the buck back up onto the trail where his final dash began, I propped open the abdomen with a short stick to let the cooling air circulate, then slowly hunted my way back toward the house. On the way, I realized this was the first animal I had taken with Dad's little Remington model 600 .308. In fact, I didn't recall Dad ever shooting anything with it other than targets. Dad would have been pleased to know it was finally put to good use filling our freezer. Hopefully, my daughters will eventually get back into hunting someday, and one of them will shoot a deer with it too. Maybe even my granddaughter will put it to her shoulder in a future quest to fill the freezer. God willing, I'll get to put it to use at least a few more times myself.

I felt the cold breeze on my face as I made my way back up to our house, but its only effect was to assure me that my venison was cooling like it should. It was the day before Thanksgiving, but I was plenty thankful already. I sent a picture of my first UP buck to a friend of mine, Jeff Scott. He commented how he liked the cedar-colored antlers. I liked that description—*cedar-colored*. It was fitting for a buck that likely spent a good deal of time in the cedar swamp on the north end of our woods. Those cedar-colored antlers now sit on the windowsill above my desk. Sometimes I lean back in my chair and gaze at them with a glassy-eyed stare while I'm out chasing hoofprints in my mind.

Skiing the Road

*Winter's wind may sting your skin, but
its soft beauty warms your heart.*

Like many January days in the north country, it was overcast but
not really cloudy. Our thermometer read 40 degrees Fahrenheit,
which is warm by cross-country skiing standards, but it was our first
good opportunity to ski since moving to the Upper Peninsula in late
November. Snow accumulation had a few recent setbacks, so there
was only about eight inches in the woods—four inches on the seasonal road alongside of our property where we would be skiing. I
debated in my head whether it would even be worth it or not. We
would have to use that bubblegum wax for warm, wet snow—the

gooey red stuff that stays on your hands like pine sap. Not what you would expect for a January afternoon in the central Upper Peninsula, but we were anxious to ski, so we figured we might as well give it a shot. After all, cross-country skiing was one of the reasons we chose to move here. Well, that and snowshoeing, trout fishing, agate hunting, hiking… It's a long list. Anyway, there was no reason not to go. So we dug out our gear and, after rubbing the red mess of goo off my hands, headed off down the driveway.

The first mile or so of road was plowed and icy, but it had just enough fresh snow cover along the edge to make skiing possible. Gliding was easy. Kicking was not. But being my first time on skis in a long time, it felt good. I couldn't recall if we even got to ski at all the previous year when we were living downstate. Maybe once. It would have to have been an evening ski right after a day of snow because, by morning, it would have been melting.

A pine squirrel dashed to a scraggly cedar along the edge of our property. It caught me by surprise, being the first one I had seen at our new place. All the rest had been black and gray squirrels so far. I've since come to find that the majority of the squirrels around our property are red squirrels, but that first one caught my interest.

Surprisingly, I fell into a comfortable skiing rhythm right off. It's not always like that the first time you do something after a long time away. For instance, our first canoe trip each season usually starts out with a lot of unsynchronized, splashy paddling before we finally settle into a groove. Skiing typically works the same way. The first couple of miles are not pretty. Muscles that I haven't flexed in a while usually start off with a burn too. But it was not so that first day. I felt like I would expect to feel at the end of a good skiing season. Trees slid steadily by, spruce and hemlock, white pine, soft maple, birch… never mind. No need to keep track. This outing wasn't for detailed observations or amateur scientific studies, just skiing. Kick, glide, breathe in the north woods, absorb the surroundings, kick, glide…

Three miles literally slid by smoothly except for the couple of times I stopped to make sure my wife, Julie, was still behind me. That's when the wet snow and assorted debris would cling to the bottom of my skis. I would have to scuff it off before settling back into my rhythm again. No matter. Kick, glide, breathe…

The DNR access point we had set as our destination (to scout for spring kayaking opportunities) was surrounded by a hedge of thick tag alders. It was close to Lake Superior, close enough that I could catch a few glimpses through the brush. There were no clear views to see what it really looked like, just a few teasing peeks. It was getting late in the day. Superior would have to be another time, hopefully soon, but another time. Another time and another adventure. It was comforting to know that there would be other times and other adventures. Again, that's why we moved here. For that evening, though, we pointed our skis back toward home. Kick, glide, breathe…

That was the first of many skiing outings along the seasonal road by our house. Not that it's our favorite place to ski or anything. It's just convenient, and it travels through some pretty property. It's easy skiing, and we hardly ever see anyone else, so we can just ski. We know what's coming up ahead (usually), so we're not looking for anything in particular, just getting fresh air and exercise while gliding through white pines, hemlocks, spruce, cedar, and a host of north woods trees. There is a special paper birch we always enjoy. Its bark seems more snow white than most. Branches dip down, then curve upward, making them look more like arms than mere branches. It stands alone, right at the road's edge, backdropped by a bog of tamarack, spruce, and tag alder. I encountered an ermine at its base one day, but it captured my attention even before that. It had a personality. Not that other trees didn't, but this one stood out from the crowd or, I suppose more appropriately, the forest. We typically stop and visit when we pass, or we at least slow down and take notice.

The road—or *our* road, as we think of it—provides an avenue for monitoring local wildlife activity, especially deer, as we're always on the lookout for tracks crossing the road, or at least I am. I especially like seeing deer tracks in the dead of winter as it's an indication that things are not too severe and the local deer herd is still out and about instead of holed up in the deer yard.

Skiing our side road also allows us to keep tabs on what the Laughing Whitefish River is up to, at least at the two crossing points and down near the mouth. Through most of ski season, the stretch of river right behind our property is usually hidden beneath a blanket of ice and snow, which sometimes acts as a highway for the wildlife we're keeping an eye on too. Farther downstream, though, there's faster water that is often open a good share of the winter. I like to stop and watch tannin water flowing over submerged ice and listen to the small rapids singing just west of the bridge.

Open, easy skiing along our road gives me the opportunity to slip into autopilot and let my mind wander. It gives me time to think, ponder, and dream while I'm in motion. I relive other, more wilderness skiing adventures. Sometimes I'm back in graduate school at Michigan Tech, and Julie is following me through the winding, rugged trails south of Lake Fanny Hooe near Copper Harbor, which was one of our favorite weekend haunts. We're watching bald eagles or following otter tracks. Then I may revisit the Porcupine Mountains backcountry, ski touring with my college friend Billy B. We're trying to follow summer trails hidden beneath a few feet of winter, crossing flowing rivers on fallen trees and setting up camp in a subzero sunset. Eventually, I'm back on the road someplace other than where I was last time I noticed and wondering what I missed.

Although roads are certainly not my favorite places to cross-country ski, there was one other memorable road skiing adventure in our past. When we lived in Houghton, while I was in graduate school at Michigan Tech, Julie and I skied Brockway Mountain Drive from just outside of Copper Harbor up to the observation area on top and back down again. On a recent drive along that same route, I was amazed that anyone would ski it, especially on regular old cross-country skis. You would think an engineer (or even an engineering student) would be smarter than that. But that was during our early twenties, in our invincible stage, back in 1987 or '88.

It was the type of winter day we had come to expect in the Keweenaw—semi-overcast sky with off-and-on flurries carried by a slight northwesterly breeze. The ski up wasn't so much skiing as it was just climbing while wearing skis. There were a few small downhill dips higher up where we actually glided for a brief stretch, but mostly it was a lot of short choppy steps, herring-boning and side-stepping. There were also a "few" rest breaks in the mix, but we didn't bother to count how many. Most of the road was well packed due to snowmobile traffic, which we were on constant lookout for. We could have just hiked up carrying our skis, but then, technically, we wouldn't have been able to say we skied up Brockway Mountain. I don't recall how long it actually took us to reach the top. The years tend to erase those types of memories. I do vaguely recall questioning the sanity of the venture a few times, and I assume Julie did as well. But neither of us actually verbalized the thought, so on we went, both probably thinking the other must be confident this was a good idea. It's funny how reasonable and matter-of-fact ventures like this seem during planning.

I think the planning discussion went like this:

"Hey, we should cross-country ski Brockway Mountain Drive this weekend," and Julie replied.

"Okay, that sounds like fun."

Or something to that effect.

Emerging from the trees onto the bare, rounded peak felt abrupt. Within a few steps or, in this case, strides, the tree cover was gone, and we were confronted with the bite of a Superior wind across the stark openness. In one way we wanted to linger, soaking in the vastness of the view, but then again part of us missed the comforting sheltered feeling of the trees. We lingered. We couldn't help it. Around the small loop we went, counterclockwise, just like when we follow the signs in our truck, taking in the view from every direction. Unlike on a clear, open-water day, to the north was just white. I knew there were details in the rolling snowscape and sharp pressure ridges of Superior, but from our vantage point, it was white.

Gazing west, I recognized shoreline features near Eagle Harbor. Then I found myself staring down the backbone of the Keweenaw, wondering at the details hidden in the trees and ridges. In situations like this, I find myself wanting to go there and see. I want the unknown landscape to be familiar. Maybe another adventure on another day. I put it on my "maybe someday" list and moved my focus south across the wooded hills and creases toward Lake Madora. That lake always caught my attention and imagination whenever we drove past on our way to or from Copper Harbor, not unlike that day. It was already on my "maybe someday" list. Standing there, I had no way of knowing that someday would be more than thirty years distant, and I would be gazing intently back in the opposite direction from an orange kayak, bobbing on the choppy surface, as I was finally familiarizing myself with the details of Lake Madora. That's part of the fun of a "someday" list. There is no time limit, and you've always got things to fuel your dreams.

Turning east there was Copper Harbor, Lake Fanny Hooe and the rugged wooded trails we sometimes explored on those same skis. Beyond lay what was, for me, the uncharted ground of the tip of the Keweenaw. It, too, was already on my list and would be for a number of years. Sometimes dreams just need time to mature. Or maybe we do.

As the sting of an unchecked breeze became more noticeable, we decided it was time to begin our descent. It's funny how much more menacing hills look from the top. The old boots that fit the bindings on my wide, no-wax touring skis were out of commission, so I was wearing the only other skis I had, thin waxable racing skis. I knew they were fast, but I had never experienced a relatively smooth wide hill where I could let them reach their true potential. The speed surprised me and got me wondering if my own potential matched the skis. The wind from my downward momentum caused my eyes to water. Blurred vision, added to my surprising sense of acceleration, began to unnerve me a bit as I sped over a section of jumbled snowmobile tracks. As my speed decreased going up the first knoll in the rolling roadway, confidence crept back in. It was destined for a short life, though.

The next grade was a little more substantial, a little steeper, a little longer, and I came to find out that it had a few more meandering snowmobile tracks as well. About three-quarters of the way down that slope, I encountered one of those vagabond tracks angling toward the shoulder of the hardpacked road. My left ski decided to follow it. Sensing the sideways tug on my ski, I glanced down in time to watch my left ski tip cross over the right. I had just enough time to think "Oh!" before I found myself testing the firmness of the snowpack. It was more like a downhill skiing wipeout than a cross-country skiing fall. Skis and poles departed and ventured off on their own, followed by my knit hat. To me, it was just a couple seconds of blur, but Julie said it was quite a show. Fortunately, there were no other spectators, but I checked as I got up just to be sure. After brushing off most of my snow collection, I gathered my belongings and my wits, in that order, and continued on, a little shaken but not admitting it.

The remainder of the slopes I took much more cautiously, especially the final one that steeply snaked its way down to highway M-26. If nothing else, the day was certainly a memorable adventure, but we've never repeated it. In fact, that's probably the only skiing adventure that we haven't repeated at least once. I'm not sure if that's because we're losing our sense of daring adventure as we get older or we're just getting smarter. We'll go with smarter.

Vertical Ice Adventures

*Sometimes, living on the edge is the best way
to get to the center of existence.*

I hadn't climbed ice since my college days, which I sometimes have difficulty admitting (even to myself) was more than thirty years ago. But when my wife, Julie, and I moved back up to Michigan's Upper Peninsula and found a nice place to live only thirty minutes from Munising, home to the Michigan Ice Fest, I couldn't resist the chance to get back in the harness again and do some ice climbing.

It was all fun and exciting when Julie and I registered in December and the mid-February event was still several weeks away. It was even more fun pulling out my old climbing equipment and reliving some of my youthful adventures as January slowly shuffled by. But as the early days of February started ticking off the calendar, a few wisps of concern started mingling with the excitement. At fifty-five years old, I wasn't exactly in my prime anymore. I've always been active, but was I active enough for something like this? I have never been one to do things part way, so instead of easing back in by just hanging around with the climbing crowd, watching presentations, and trying out some new gear on the open climbing demo days, I signed up for an all-day Pictured Rocks Backcountry Adventure. Rumor had it we'd be hiking in and climbing Bridalveil Falls, one of the tall iconic falls along the exposed shoreline of Superior.

These types of climbs weren't new to me by any means. During my college days at Michigan Tech, I spent four winters avidly scaling similar ice formations along the Keweenaw's Superior coastal cliffs. As an active member of the Ridge Roamers Club on campus, some of us spent nearly every winter weekend climbing. The shoreline formations near Freda and Redridge were our home ice. That's where I initially learned to climb using mostly borrowed and makeshift equipment. None of us had special climbing boots. We just used our heavy leather hiking boots, the same ones I trudged around campus in every day throughout the winter. My dad cut out a pair of plexiglass plates the shape of my boots, which I sandwiched between my boot soles and crampons to increase the stiffness of the boots.

I remember Superior looking like an arctic wasteland of jumbled pressure ridges and wind-driven snow crystals. The vertical ice, though, was different. Some formations were plain paraffin-wax white, but most were varying shades of tannin amber, iron red, and exotic blue. Tucked in behind some formations were dimly lit sanctuaries from the biting wind. There you could sometimes hear a muffled chorus of running water emanating from somewhere within the ice. There was plenty to ponder and marvel at, but in those days of youth, I mostly just wanted to climb.

Early in the season, Superior typically wasn't frozen. Usually, just a portion of the small bays housing some of the climbs held lake ice, so you couldn't walk into the climbs. More often than not, we would have to rappel into the bays and climb back out. There were times we would push the season window a bit, and water would run out of ice axe holes. I also remember a few times kicking my boot through the ice to a wet foot. As a college-age guy, it was all just a part of the adventure. We just laughed it off and continued climbing.

Periodically, my friend Bill and I would go out climbing for the weekend. There was a cave in one of the cliffs where we climbed. The floor of the cave was Lake Superior, but it was shallow enough that it always froze solid. We would climb all day Saturday, typically in gale-force winds driving highly abrasive snow crystals, sleep in the cave on a bed of ice and snow Saturday night, climb for a while Sunday, and then head for town Sunday evening to study for Monday classes. Our zero-degree-rated sleeping bags certainly earned their keep, as did all our equipment in those conditions. I remember waking up one morning with snow pelting me in the face a dozen feet into the cave. We rolled over and snuggled back into our sleeping bags a while longer just for good measure. I don't recall much climbing being accomplished that day. For some reason, I also don't remember anyone else ever joining us in those campouts.

In preparation for Ice Fest, I had been doing some reconnaissance at Downwind Sports in Marquette, hosts of the Pictured Rocks Festival, talking to staff and checking out the new gear. Wow, thirty years of modification and improvement had significantly transformed most of the gear. Fortunately, for a very modest fee, I could rent new gear as part of the festival, so I didn't have to go out and buy all the new stuff, although it was tempting. I did buy a climbing guidebook for the Munising area, though, which showcased over eighty different climbs by my count. Even professional climbers, with international experience, that come for the festival consider Pictured Rocks to be a great ice climbing area.

My backcountry adventure was scheduled for Thursday, so Julie and I picked up demo (rental) gear on Wednesday just to give me a chance to get a feel for the gear by going out to some of the climbs outside of town, along Sand Point Road, and doing a little low-level playing, meaning just a few feet off the ground—climbing but not really. It felt great to be on the ice again, even at that level. Thursday was looking promising.

I had plenty of time Thursday morning to talk to our two instructors and the other six participants. Our lead instructor, Jeff Witt, typically guided climbs in the Tetons and other areas out west. Our local instructor, Colten Moore, had been climbing in the area for a number of years and was part of the Ice Fest staff. It turned out that most of the other participants had some sort of recent climbing experience. In fact, most had participated in guided events of some kind the previous day. So I was the only one with no truly recent experience, which didn't exactly give my confidence a boost. Lake Superior wasn't frozen, so there was no access to the bottom of the climb and nowhere for people to stand around there either. That being the case, we were informed that they'd be lowering us one at a time from the top, then belaying us (supporting us with the rope) from the top as well. That meant, once we were lowered over the edge, the only way out would be to climb. I took a deep breath, grabbed my gear, and got in the shuttle van.

Talking to the instructors and other participants in the shuttle eased my mind. They were all easygoing and just looking forward to a fun climbing adventure. During the snowmobile portion of the shuttle in to Miner's Beach parking area, where our hike would begin, I finally settled into adventure mode, where nervousness and concern are outweighed by excitement and anticipation, which is always a great feeling. From the parking lot, it was only a five-minute hike to Potato Patch Campground area, where we'd be doing a warm-up climb. The climb was a ten-foot diameter pillar not more than about twenty feet tall, which gave Jeff and Colton a chance to give some demonstrations and offer pointers as they watched each of us climb. Compared to what I was used to using, the new gear was like a stealthy fighter jet compared to a biplane. The biggest improvement was that the axes didn't smash my knuckles against the ice, which I appreciated. Implementing the pointers and demonstrations Jeff and Colten offered up amplified the gear improvements even more. The thirty-year climbing gap flowed away like the trickle of water coming out of the bottom of the ice pillar, and I was excited to move on to Bridalveil for the main focus of the day.

Hiking to Bridalveil took roughly another twenty minutes. The trail had been packed by the previous days' class, so snowshoes weren't needed, which was good, given that I had opted not to bring mine. It was a gorgeous sunny day with virtually no wind and temperatures hovering around 30 degrees Fahrenheit. It was not your typical winter day for the Lake Superior shoreline but was a great day to do some ice climbing—a great day to do anything outside.

At the top of Bridalveil, Jeff and Colten talked us through how they were doing the setup, which was familiar to me from my previous experience. When Colten asked who wanted to be first, I waited a couple of seconds out of general courtesy, but when nobody else volunteered, I jumped in before I lost the opportunity. Due to the dangers of getting too close to the edge of the cliff without being attached to a rope, I had no idea of exactly what the ice formation looked like until I was stepping off the brink, fully committed to whatever was to come. As I went over the lip, walking backward down the frozen falls, my fears and concerns were gone. Adventurous excitement took over. Three decades felt more like a few days ago. Though everything was new (the ice, the location, the equipment), it had a familiar feel. I kept going down until I hit the transition from vertical ice to cascading frozen snow. As Colten switched over from lowering mode to belay mode, I snapped a few quick pictures, then gazed up the climb in anticipation. I was well acquainted with the view and with that feeling of butterflies dancing in my stomach that accompanied it.

Maybe it was the excitement, maybe it was the recently acquired techniques and new equipment, but the climb was over in a few minutes. Or at least that was the way it felt. A little later, I had an opportunity to repeat the climb following a slightly different route and had the same results. I was surprised to find that I was actually climbing better than in my college days. It could've been the adrenaline, but it was most likely a result of me now relying more on efficient technique than youthful brute force. I came to realize that my earlier concerns about my current climbing ability were only in my head. Like most limitations, it turned out to be a self-imposed, imaginary wall made of doubts cemented together with fear. As soon as fear was removed, the wall of doubts crumbled.

In my early climbing days, there was a lot of axe swinging, ice spraying, arm work. Feeling fatigued and having the shakes at the end of a climb were a common theme. Numb hands and rubber arms were not unusual in those days. The new feeling was just a calming sense of having had a good outdoor workout with a slight jitter of excitement. As a bonus, my knuckles weren't bloodied and bruised either.

I had originally set out to revisit an old passion and, to a certain degree, maybe prove to myself that I hadn't lost too much ground to the turning of calendar pages. I wanted to face the challenge of vertical ice again and experience the thrill of living on the edge. My life hadn't exactly become ordinary, but it was beginning to feel a little too ordinary for my liking. Maybe moving back to the UP after a major job loss had me yearning for youthful days of raw adventure when things weren't quite so complicated. At the end of the day, I felt I had accomplished something, even though I wasn't quite sure exactly what.

As we hiked through sunlit woods back to the trailhead, shadows were beginning to lengthen, but the blue sky remained virtually unmarred, and the slight breeze still wasn't raising a legitimate whitecap on the open lake. Still not your average UP day in February, but my thoughts weren't on the weather anyway. I was thankful to be able to reconnect with the UP and Superior, contentedly looking forward to a new life of outdoor adventures. Actually, a new life. Period.

When I first signed up to participate in Ice Fest, my oldest daughter, Amy, asked me in a somewhat skeptical tone of voice if I was planning to seriously get back into this ice climbing thing. I just laughed and said that I didn't have any big plans. It was just something fun to do, partially for old time's sake. Trekking through the late-afternoon woods, with Superior stretching north to the horizon, feeling like an honest-to-goodness adventurer, I thought, *Yeah, I can see myself getting back into this.*

Sugaring

*Sap, clear as spring water, dripping from a spile, making a soft
"tink" as it splashes into a dented galvanized bucket. Crackling
flames dance across the bottom of a steel pan as sweet steam
rises from the bubbling surface of caramelizing brew. Slow
is the transition to nectar the color of a tannin-tinged North
Woods stream. Sugar Maples give their late-winter gift.*

Up north in general and in the Upper Peninsula specifically, if
you have a decent collection of sugar maples—or hard maples,
as they're known in lumbering circles—you're pretty much obligated
to operate a sugar bush to make maple syrup. Sugaring operations
certainly vary in size and complexity, ranging from a dozen or so taps
with boiling being done on the kitchen stove to upwards of 1,500

taps with a dedicated sugar shack and commercial-grade equipment. Our operation is somewhere on the lower end of mid range. More specifically, it's 53 taps and a couple of stainless-steel syrup pans on makeshift cinder block hearths housing a wood fire.

We've been doing this for more than twenty years, so we've got some experience under our belts. Still, I wouldn't say that we've got it down to a science because we tend to rely more on old-school methods than special equipment or technology.

To start with, we still use old cast-metal taps—or spiles, as they're called—and galvanized buckets with galvanized A-frame covers, just like you see in old pictures. We bought the stuff used, so we have no idea how old any of it actually is. During the boiling process, we determine when the syrup's done based on volume and what the boil looks like instead of hydrometers and such. And for packaging, we simply use standard canning jars instead of plastic jugs or fancy bottles.

When we got started making maple syrup on our farm downstate, tapping trees usually started sometime in the late February to early March time frame. Here in the UP, it's typically more like middle of March to early April. In our operation, buckets are randomly scattered through the woods around our house. So to collect the sap, which takes place once or twice each day there is a "run" of sap, I follow a self-made, somewhat-packed foot trail that serpentines from tree to tree in a route that I've deemed orderly. Being that I sometimes need to empty sap buckets after dark using a headlamp, I've found that following the same route every time on a well-packed trail is important. Otherwise, it's hard to know which buckets you've emptied and which ones you have not. It's also difficult to be sure you've emptied all the buckets if you don't follow some sort of system. Leaving buckets unemptied could mean either an overflow or that a bucket may get too heavy and pull out the spile. Either way, it wastes precious sap and puts the syrup maker in a bad mood.

The "well-packed" state of the trail, of course, depends on several factors, like snow depth, temperature, recent thawing and freezing activity, and how much sap is in the gathering buckets. Numerous times I've done a one-legger through the snow crust while collecting sap if the trail isn't packed well enough. Having one foot suddenly disappear down past the knee while carrying two five-gallon buckets of sap makes it difficult to keep from falling or even seriously splashing. In his book *The Grasshopper Trap*, Patrick F. McManus has a detailed discussion on falling. He claims that coming up with a comically droll comment with which to describe your injuries is a critical part of a successful fall—spilling sap certainly counts as an injury. While discussing the one-legger specifically, he later goes on to note that the person doing the one-legger almost always omits the comically droll comment and goes right to serious cussing. Now I don't want to dispute Pat's astute observations, nor do I want to incriminate myself, but I do have to admit that I don't ever remember making a comically droll comment after doing a one-legger, especially while carrying a couple of five-gallon buckets full of sap. That's all I'm going to say.

So after collecting the sap, I store it in food-grade 55-gallon barrels until I have enough to boil. For me, "enough" is at least 60 gallons because, at roughly a 40:1 ratio (40 gallons of sap to make 1 gallon of syrup), 60 gallons is the least amount that I can boil all the way down to syrup without it getting too shallow in the pan and scorching. I have two pans, so I can readily boil up to 120 gallons. Processing beyond 120 gallons just takes way too long, so I usually try to boil before I get much over 120 gallons of sap stored in my barrels. Quite often, I end up missing that goal and have to accept the fact that it's going to be a long day (or night) of boiling.

Just to give you an idea of timing, a 60-gallon batch typically takes about 9 hours to boil down. I say *typically*. If I'm not on the ball, keeping the fire stoked enough to produce a constant rolling boil in the pan, then it can easily slide into 10 or 11 hours. So I have plenty of time to think and ponder things while I'm out boiling sap, although I've found that, after about midnight, extra thinking time doesn't really get put to good use. In fact, that's pretty much the case after 8 or 9 hours of boiling, regardless of the time of day.

Over the two seasons that I've been making maple syrup here in the UP, I've noticed that it consistently takes about 1.5 times as long as it did when we made syrup downstate in the Jackson area. I do recall reading somewhere that traveling north has a similar effect on boiling time as gaining elevation. I've never bothered to follow up on the science behind that claim, but I've certainly found it to be true, especially with boiling sap. Besides, when it's 3:00 or 4:00 a.m. and you've been boiling since 9:00 a.m. the previous morning, you don't really give a rip about the science. You're just tired of boiling. For that matter, boiling has nothing to do with it. You're just tired. This is exactly why we don't do the final process of filtering and canning right after the primary boiling. More often than not, we let the syrup cool in a couple of stainless-steel stock pots for anywhere from a few hours to a couple of days, depending on our schedule. The downside is that we have to take time to reheat the syrup on the kitchen stove, where we do our final processing. The upside is that my attitude is much better at that point. I've found it's best to let attitude trump saving a little extra time and propane.

Sometimes it can be difficult to gauge the depth of liquid in a 2 ft. × 3 ft. pan with steam rolling off the surface and swirls of wood smoke burning your eyes. So the other way I gauge when the batch is done is by watching it boil. I've found that when it crosses the line between sap and syrup, the boil characteristics change from normal boiling (like water) to more of a foamy boil. It may not be very scientific or sophisticated, but it works. Pretty well anyway. Again, between steam and smoke, boiling details aren't always crystal clear either, so I tend to err on the conservative side and let it go until I'm sure it's syrup, which is why our syrup is often a little thicker and sweeter than traditional maple syrup. Or maybe I should say it's thicker and sweeter than commercial maple syrup to be more accurate.

I happen to like thicker, sweeter maple syrup, so I'm happy. You do lose a little volume of syrup when you err on the conservative side like this, but we're primarily making it for our own use, so I'm fine with going for what I consider to be higher quality and give up a little quantity. That being said, there have been a couple of incidents, though, where I waited to the point of a serious foam-up. When the syrup cooled, it was the consistency of honey. It was great on pancakes and ice cream, but it was a major pain to filter. I wouldn't suggest going that far on purpose unless you're trying to make sugar.

Once you get started, sugaring is one of those endeavors that you just can't give up even though it's a lot of work and it can be pretty dirty working with those sooty pans. You also have to put up with a lot of smoke. In fact, I can usually still smell smoke a day (or even sometimes two) after boiling. It permeates your skin. There are worse smells you could have to deal with, though. So the wood smoke issue doesn't bother me. Besides, I like the smell of wood smoke.

Making maple syrup takes dedication. In some ways, on a superficial level, the time and effort invested in making your own maple syrup the old-fashioned way is far greater than the gain, but somehow, for some reason, it's addicting, like gardening or raising your own meat. Once you get started, you have to keep doing it. You just can't seem to give it up, even if in some ways you want to. But maybe it's not the process of sugaring that's so addictive. Maybe it's the syrup itself. If you couldn't tell, I love maple syrup. It's one of those sweet gifts God provides through nature. Besides being used on pancakes and waffles, it's great on oatmeal, yogurt, and ice cream, just to mention a few. Sometimes, I will dribble some on my bagel before I spread the cream cheese. Other times, I don't bother with the cream cheese. We often cook with it too. But still, there's more to it than just the physical attraction to the syrup end product, even though precious gifts like that are hard to walk away from. There's something about the sugaring process itself that just pulls you in. It's hard to quit, even at the end of a good, long season.

One season a number of years ago, the conditions were just right for the better part of a month, and sap flowed freely. Day after day, it just kept coming. We made twenty-five gallons of syrup that year, boiling over a thousand gallons of sap in our small backyard operation. I was working a full-time job and still staying up all night boiling two nights a week. Then I boiled most of the weekend, four weekends in a row. It was all I could do to keep up. The entire month was just a blur of boiling sap, not to mention the collecting and canning. I felt, and probably looked, like I had taken a long-distance red-eye flight every night for a month.

One day when the season was about over, I told my wife, Julie, that I didn't know how long I could keep this up.

Looking at me like I was an adolescent in need of direction, she asked, "Why don't you just pull all the taps and stop?" Somehow, in my maple-syrup-junkie frenzy, I hadn't thought of that.

Conserving the Wild U.P.

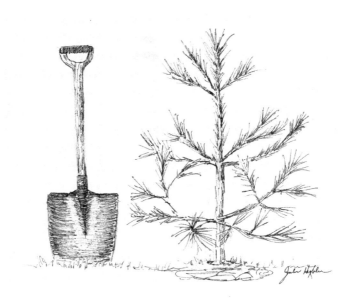

Superior mysteries are many. Pondering them is time well spent. Preserving them would be a lifetime well spent.

My wife, Julie, and I hadn't been on a legitimate hike in quite a while. I don't recall exactly how long it had been, but it was too long for our liking. This was a typical August day for our neck of the woods, sunny and mildly warm, with a light breeze blowing in off the Big Lake. There were a few flying insects of the blood-sucking variety but not enough to be an issue. So we decided to head over to the Pictured Rocks National Lakeshore, with our sights set on the scenic loop in to Chapel Rock, then along the Superior shoreline to Mosquito Beach, and back to the car by way of the Mosquito River and falls. It's a popular area, but we figured if we left soon, we would be there by midmorning, which should beat a majority of the crowd.

It all sounded like a good plan, as plans often do, but at the end of the five-mile dirt access road, we found the roughly fifty-vehicle parking lot completely full. There were vehicles parked along both sides of the road the last couple of hundred yards before the parking area, and at least eight other vehicles were following us in. With a grunt of disgust, I looped through the lot and headed back to the main road. I don't recall if I said much of anything, but if I did, I'm sure it's not worth repeating.

We managed to salvage our plans for a hike by heading farther east to the Beaver Basin Wilderness. Beaver Basin is still part of the park, but being a little less accessible, it wasn't nearly as crowded.

That incident, and others like it, have gotten me thinking about the pressures a lot of our natural areas like the Pictured Rocks are experiencing. Here in the UP, because nature's wildness is so readily available and accessible, it's also vulnerable and showing signs of wear and tear. The good news is that the popularity of wild places means that people—lots of people—want contact with the wild. Brushes with the wild fill a gap in our modern lives. Some people may be able to honestly claim no interest or connection to wild things and wild places, but most of us cannot. For some of us, connections with wild things and wild places are a daily occurrence. In fact, it's a daily necessity, like eating. Both provide sustenance that keeps us going. I've visited cities across the country. Even though they may contain interesting shops, museums, and historical buildings, I always find myself drawn to their parks and caged street-side trees, where I feel more connected and at home.

So if the vast majority of Americans feel at least some attraction to or connection with wild places and wild things, why are the majority of Americans not actively involved in conserving these places? Apathy? Ignorance? Lack of understanding the true situation? Or maybe they are just busy and figure that there are agencies and organizations out there just for that purpose. They probably figure that those other people will take care of it—"it" meaning anything from picking up litter to maintaining trails to restoring watersheds.

Government agencies and conservation organizations are great, and they are doing much-needed work, but they cannot possibly do it all. It's up to private citizens, especially when you consider that the bulk of land is in private ownership. Individuals need to take responsibility and take charge. Learn about invasive species, and take up the fight to hold them back. Learn about native species, and work to help them thrive on a local level. Be good stewards. We need to become the majority. If a majority of the population become good stewards, then each of us will not have such a daunting job to do.

Fly-fishing author John Gierach, in his book titled *Even Brook Trout Get the Blues*, says, "You must be an environmental activist at some level—there's no way around it that'll still let you live with yourself—but you should never get so grim about it that you stop enjoying what you're supposed to be fighting for."

I don't consider myself an activist. I'm what I would call a conservationist. Even though it may just sound like semantics, to me, it makes a difference. For the most part, I connect activists with politics, and I just don't want to go there. But there are times when you really can't avoid getting into politics to some degree if you want to help keep our environment from getting completely trampled.

Conservationists, on the other hand, I see as more hands-on workers. They base their projects and battles on facts and figures from scientific data. Yeah, I'm sure emotions come into play but only in a supporting role, not the main driver. I may be wrong, and I don't doubt these comments will rub some people the wrong way, but that's the way I see it. Now that I've said all that, it probably doesn't really matter because, in many cases, we're fighting for the same things—to protect our natural landscapes and natural communities and to restore those areas that have already been degraded to some degree or another.

One of the big conservation issues is the battle with invasive species. Some invasive species are easy to want to eradicate, like Japanese knotweed, because it's not that pretty and it's obviously destructive as it breaks up foundations and walkways. Others are not so easy to despise—forget-me-nots, for instance. Even though they're considered an invasive here in the UP, my wife loves them, which probably goes back to the summer we spent in Alaska early in our marriage. Forget-me-nots are Alaska's state flower. I have to admit they're beautiful and easy to love, but they're not native to the UP, and they spread like wildfire.

I remember the first summer in our UP home seeing a few sparse forget-me-not plants in the edge of our yard. That was before I knew they were invasive. The next summer, there were numerous healthy-looking patches all around our yard, in the lawn, and along the road. Late in the season, I found out through the Alger County Conservation District, to my wife's dismay, that they were invasive, so I started pulling them. I obviously didn't do a thorough job because, in the third season, they were even more plentiful. I almost hate to pull them because they are so pretty, but I can see where this situation is going. Now I pull them whenever my wife's not looking and toss them in our burn barrel for incineration. I try to leave just enough where Julie can see them to keep her happy while still trying to keep them under control. So far, it's working out all right. I'm maintaining family peace while still feeling like I'm doing my job as a conservationist. In the back of my mind, though, my conservationist conscience is bothering me a bit for not pulling them all, so I'm not quite sure how this story is going to play out.

One of the things I've found about conservation issues is that once you learn about them, you see them everywhere. Spotted knapweed is a good example. Somehow, I never realized that spotted knapweed was an invasive species. It's probably because it's so prevalent, so I've always just assumed that it belongs here. It doesn't. Now that I know that and understand why that's a problem, I see it everywhere. I can't get away from the stuff. Spotted knapweed plants are the cigarette butts of the plant world. I see them everywhere I look, especially along roadsides. I can't possibly address the issue along every road in the Upper Peninsula, but I can certainly address it right where I live. Our property is at an intersection, so counting both roads, we have about a mile of roadside. I took up the battle a couple of years ago and started pulling the plants before they went to seed. I haven't managed to eradicate it yet, but I'm making noticeable progress.

On the other side of the coin, I had an opportunity to get involved with a grant to improve deer habitat by planting native trees and shrubs. Even though our property was already pretty good habitat, there's usually room for improvement. The idea was to increase thermal cover by planting some white pines and then enhance the future food supply by adding oaks, hazelnuts, high-bush cranberries, and a variety of apples. Besides benefiting deer and other wildlife, I got a fringe benefit out of the deal too. By roaming our property, searching out good planting sites, I ended up exploring our property much more thoroughly than usual, which provided a much better understanding of our place. I also discovered some tiny hidden forest openings and clues to deer activities and usage I previously didn't know. The planting process benefited me along with our local wildlife. The more I know and understand our property, the better job I can do enhancing and protecting it. The same goes for public property as well. The more we know and understand it, the more we can enjoy it, and the more likely we are to be good stewards of it. By knowing it more intimately, we will also better understand how to best take care of it. So my constant and seemingly random explorations do have a purpose, and that's the story I'm sticking with.

Getting back to those conservation organizations I noted earlier, there are plenty to choose from. I'm personally involved with several to one extent or another, but I'll refrain from naming them here so as not to imply a bias. The important thing is to connect with an organization that is truly doing hands-on conservation and is working in an area that touches your heart. Get involved in something that you're honestly passionate about. I've found that working on things I'm passionate about is much more than just rewarding; it's fun. Maybe more importantly, it's energizing. Energy breeds excitement, and excitement is contagious. It just can't help spreading.

It may be hard to believe, but I often get as much satisfaction and enjoyment out of conservation projects and activities as I do from things like hiking, fishing, or paddling. They all take me outside and help me connect with our natural world. Probably just as important, those activities also provide opportunities to connect with other conservation-minded people. The other benefit is that those same activities also provide opportunities to interact and connect with non-conservation-minded people. My hope is for those interactions and connections to help more people understand the need for conservation. Ultimately, they will hopefully not only understand the need for conservation but the need for them to become actively involved in conservation as well. That's where the contagious excitement and energy comes in. People are drawn to those things and want to be active participants, which is good not only for conservation but for those people themselves. Many people say that being connected with our natural world and working to conserve it fill a void in their life. I believe that's because we were created to be an integral part of the natural world and to be caretakers of it, not just distant spectators.

Albert Einstein is noted to have said that you cannot expect to be able to solve a problem with the same level of effort that went into creating it. That is painfully true for conservation. With the number of people and organizations that have contributed to creating the many environmental issues we're facing today, a relatively small number of conservation organizations and conservation-minded individuals cannot possibly hope to correct all these situations. Conservation needs a community—a large and passionate community.

We always need at least one more person contributing to the solution instead of the problem.

One of my big conservation concerns is the recent decline in hunting and fishing. Here in Michigan, as in most other states, I've seen multiple sources noting that the number of people who actively hunt and fish is decreasing. One of the problems with that trend is that a large share of conservation funding comes from hunting and fishing in the form of license fees, special equipment taxes, and membership dues or donations to conservation organizations. In addition, much of the hands-on conservation work is done by those of us who hunt and fish, either through personal initiatives or being involved in a conservation-based organization. So at a time when conservation issues and opportunities are on the rise, conservation funding and physical labor for conservation projects are falling off. Other outdoor pursuits, like mountain biking and hiking, appear to be on the rise, but those activities do not really generate much, if any, financial or physical support for conservation, at least not right now. Hopefully, we'll find a way to change both the trends and funding methods in the near future.

Most likely, those changes will come from changing the way we think about conservation because conservation is really a mindset more than an activity. Once you honestly have a conservation mindset, becoming active in funding and/or doing conservation work is pretty much a given. Our society, actually our whole world, desperately needs a new conservation mindset.

As I noted earlier, I consider conservation activities to be on the same level as other outdoors passions, like hiking, skiing, hunting, and fishing. To me, the key is passion. Passion is where the deep driving desire to do something comes from. It's what creates the excitement in doing something. Passion is the fire inside that keeps us fully alive instead of merely existing. If you're truly passionate about the natural world and your endeavors there, you'll naturally want to give something back, help clean up messes, right wrongs, and stop more wrongs and messes from happening.

For me, interacting with the natural world, mingling with the rest of creation, is a passion. Whether I'm hiking trails, exploring the winter woods, chasing deer during a hunt, or exploring a stream with a fly rod, I feel fully engaged. All of my senses are running on high, and I feel like I'm right where I need to be, right where I belong. Working on conservation efforts brings on those same feelings and emotions. All those outdoor passions define who I am. By preserving those things, conserving them, in essence, I'm conserving myself. Not doing conservation work, for me, would be like not exploring, hunting, or fishing—in other words, not living.

I'll be actively involved in outdoor pursuits for as long as I'm physically and mentally able. So I expect I'll be working to conserve the wild UP just as long. After that, I hope and pray that the people I've had the blessing of being a positive influence for will passionately and energetically carry on from there, until there's no longer a need. Unfortunately, my guess is that the need won't be gone until time and the earth we live on no longer exist. So we carry on with our work, content to be caretakers of the world around us, engaging our abilities and passions for something beyond ourselves.

Parting Thoughts

My experiences with the wild UP run the gamut from momentary brushes to immersions of a couple of weeks or more. I've found that, here in the UP, you don't have to look far to find the wild. As a matter of fact, in most places, if you stand still for a while, the wild, in one form or another, will probably find you.

Regardless of your abilities, to some extent, the wild UP is within everyone's reach. You'll need to put away your electronic devices, though, so you can focus on the reality at hand. Besides, in a lot of areas, cell service and internet access don't exist here anyway. Compared to what you'll experience, though, those devices really won't matter.

The UP is what seems like an endless collection of places to roam and explore, places to touch the wild and experience nature in its pure sense. It has its share of backcountry wilderness, if that's what you're seeking, but nature doesn't only exist in vast wilderness areas. The essence of wilderness is all around us, especially here in the Upper Peninsula. We often pass right by it every day without even giving it a second look—wildflowers growing along a busy highway, a meandering creek or roadside waterfall, that little trail crossing the road. The feeling of wilderness and the refreshing power of nature are there, patiently waiting for us to notice them. The thrill of nature's surprises, the feeling of peace, and the calming effects of God's natural world can be found all around us. We just need to look.

As kids, adventures abound. Natural wonders are everywhere. Anywhere there is a puddle of water, a flower, a tree, a wild adventure calls us. All too often, as we grow up, we lose that sense of wonder. The everyday spirit of adventure fades like summer vacation freedom on the first day of a new school year.

The good news is that our youthful sense of adventure usually doesn't disappear altogether. It's just buried beneath a few layers of maturity, responsibility, and other refinements we've undergone over the years. Quite often, we can feel it bubbling deep down inside when we have a brush with a potential adventure. It's that pull to poke around in that stream you pass by now and then, that unexplainable sense of peace and tranquility you feel as you watch large soft snowflakes drifting down and clinging to the trees. It shows itself in the way we're drawn to watching even the smallest of wildlife busily going about their activities in the backyard or the woodlot down the road. As we stare into a dying campfire or backyard bonfire, we feel the need to throw on one more log because we don't want the fire to go out.

The other good news is that it usually doesn't take much to get the flames of adventure going again. Throw a little tinder on those old coals, and it's not long before the flame returns. Take a walk through the nearest woods. Explore a patch of state land or national forest; there's lots of it around. Find a stream or river to explore. Even if you only have an hour to invest, it doesn't take much tinder. It doesn't take a major excursion or lots of planning because the wilds don't only exist in the wilderness. The healing benefits of nature are everywhere to be enjoyed. The rejuvenating powers are ready to lift us up and carry us on until the next time we venture out into the wild, near or far.

It seems like I'm adding new outdoor adventures to my to-do list almost on a daily basis. Just looking at a map usually sparks ideas for at least a few adventures. Taking a hike and pondering nature is good for generating ideas too. I've also found that looking at pictures or thinking about previous outings is a sure way to help bubble new plans to the surface. With everything that's on my list now, I'll likely never live long enough to accomplish them all. The benefit of that situation, though, is that I'll never be without a pending adventure as long as I live. I always have things to plan, dream about, and look forward to.

There's virtually no limit to the types of outdoors adventures or the level of intensity available here in the Upper Peninsula whether you're simply looking to get outside to get some exercise and fresh air, advance to mentally and physically challenging endeavors, or anything in between. Whether your outing is a lengthy, well-planned venture or a brief, spur-of-the-moment activity, the wild UP is always out there waiting. If you don't have plans for your next outing, now is a great time to start.

The important thing is to get out into the wild UP and play. Maybe I'll see you there.

About the Author

For more than five decades, John Highlen has been enjoying pursuits such as hiking, hunting, fishing, backpacking, canoeing, kayaking, exploring, and climbing, as well as many others. These years spent absorbed in the outdoors, experiencing nature from numerous perspectives, has given him a deep appreciation of and respect for our natural world. As a degreed mechanical engineer, John is able to recognize and understand the details of what he sees and how those details work together in the grand scheme. Overall, this eclectic blend of skills and experience allows him to see and interpret the natural world through a unique set of eyes. John strives to use those skills and experience in his writing to help connect readers with the natural world everyone is meant to be a part of and all the intrinsic benefits that flow from that connection. In 2016, John was blessed to be able to turn his attention full-time to outdoor adventures, writing, volunteering for conservation organizations, and being the support crew for his wife, Julie's art studio.

John and his wife enjoy living in Deerton, Michigan, in a home surrounded by woods, less than ten minutes from the wonders of Lake Superior. From this vantage point, they paint the wilds of the north woods and waters to share nature's inspiration with others—Julie with brush and canvas, John with pen and paper.

CPSIA information can be obtained
at www.ICGtesting.com
Printed in the USA
LVHW100705130622
721092LV00006B/461